W9-DDI-172

*The search
for meaningful
existence*

...ITY SCHOOL...
VILLAGE...

The search for meaningful existence

CHARLES B. KETCHAM

Weybright and Talley
NEW YORK

UNITY SCHOOL LIBRARY
UNITY VILLAGE, MISSOURI 64065

For Joyce

© 1968 Charles B. Ketcham

*All rights reserved, including the right
to reproduce this book or portions
thereof in any form.*

Published in the United States by
WEYBRIGHT AND TALLEY, INC.
*3 East 54th Street,
New York, New York* 10022

Published simultaneously in Canada by
CLARKE, IRWIN & COMPANY LIMITED,
Toronto and Vancouver

Library of Congress Catalog Card No. 68–28268
PRINTED IN THE UNITED STATES OF AMERICA

B
821
.K38

Foreword

The motivation for undertaking the following study of the continuity and affirmation in the intellectual-artistic-spiritual revolution of our times, came to irrepressible maturity the fifteenth time I was reminded by our culture-critics: "'Tis all in pieces, all coherence gone." It is true that we are at the end of an era, but this revolution is not called Armageddon. It is the contention of this essay that the contours of a new age and a new community are becoming evident everywhere about us. It is not so much a rebirth out of the "pieces of incoherence" as a creation, a new birth, out of man's emerging sense of what it means to *be* human. It is a new era, a new humanism, a new theology in the process of establishing its own new morality.

That a study so motivated has come to market is due to the initiative, encouragement, and generosity of Mr. Victor Weybright of Weybright and Talley, Inc. I am deeply indebted to him for this opportunity of extending a preliminary study, "The Search for the New Morality" which appeared earlier in *The Christian Century*.

v

So, too, am I indebted to my colleagues Professor Alfred Kern, Chairman of the Department of English, Allegheny College; Professor Carl Heeschen, Chairman of the Department of Art, Allegheny College; and Professor Malcolm Seagrave, Chairman of the Department of Fine Arts, Alliance College. While they in no way bear responsibility for the ideas or thesis of this essay, it was their scholarship which restrained my homiletical tendency to make extravagant claims in areas of their competence.

I am particularly grateful to my friend Professor James F. Day of the Department of Philosophy and Religion, Allegheny College, who read the manuscript of this essay and made many critical suggestions that have been incorporated in the final draft.

To two of my students, Miss Virginia Moulthrop and Miss Marianne Spitzform, I would like to acknowledge my indebtedness for their help in countless tasks of research.

Charles B. Ketcham

Ruter Hall
Allegheny College
May, 1968

Contents

. . . I am waiting
for a rebirth of wonder

*   *   *

and I am waiting
for the Age of Anxiety
to drop dead. . . .
          from "I Am Waiting"
          FERLINGHETTI

one: The loss of wonder

NOTHING HAS DISTURBED contemporary man more than the loss of his secure, sophisticated, predictable, insured little world. The double indemnity of goods and services provided by his technological age should have compensated such a loss, but, as with so much tragedy, affluence doesn't fit the crime. What man has lost, as Ferlinghetti suggests, is wonder—not worldliness.

In his commendable and historic, but single-minded, attempts to provide jobs, food, clothing, and shelter technological man seems to have lost the two things which historically have justified this concentration on material needs. One is community with his fellow man; the other is a sense of the transcendent. Affluence and productive power have given contemporary man a false sense of independence and security by substituting his functional expertise and organization for cooperative community. He knows that if he dislikes the way the "game" is being played, he can pick up his computer and plug it in somewhere else. What he fails to perceive is that without community, without an acknowledgment of a necessary and fundamental relationship with other men (and therefore responsibility for others) his personal world becomes defensive and self-centered. There is more fear than wonder in that.

With no sense of the transcendent, no acknowledgment of a creator or a creation, the technological man's world becomes purposeless—in fact absurd, for all he can detect with certainty is a pervasive hostility which plots his demise and death. Nothing but these emerge as necessary or inevitable. As a result, he is, as he is without community, defensive; for he is convinced that he lives only once, that he cannot waste time on sentimental sanctimony, and that he cannot afford the luxury of genuine (but futile) altruism. There is not much "wonder" involved in this realistic (maybe ruthless or maybe suave) egotism.

It is not a particularly attractive portrait to view, if one's attitude toward life tends toward either religious idealism or pragmatic humanism. But the fact remains: acknowledged or unacknowledged, technological man—mass man—has become paranoid. Isolated and without a cosmic identity, he has nowhere to go, nothing to achieve, and no one to believe. He is Jean-Baptiste in Camus' *The Fall* who is inclined to take himself for a prophet, "having taken refuge in a desert of stones, fogs, and stagnant waters—an empty prophet for shabby times, Elijah without a messiah, choked with fever and alcohol, my back up against this moldy door, my finger raised toward a threatening sky, showering imprecations on lawless men who cannot endure any judgment." The evidence of such awareness of world loss is all about us, and it is the sudden shock of self-conscious complicity in this knowledge that has driven so many into the search for the New Humanism.

The aspect of world loss which, if not the most shocking, is at least the most universal is the loss of continuity. Deprived of a transcendent orientation, we find that we are equally deprived of any alternative. We can no longer comprehend or understand the world in which we live. The age of computers and technological sophistication has made not only our Newtonian world (which we at least superficially comprehended) obsolete, it has even begun to introduce us to a post-Einsteinian universe at a time when most of us can only claim the vaguest notion of what Einstein's thought was all about.

As laymen in the scientific technocentric world, our only consolation is that the professionals, the scientists themselves, have likewise lost the sense of continuity. Technological languages, concepts, methodologies, and interests have become so prolific, yet so specialized and so precise, that even within a given scientific discipline there is often little communication or understanding, e.g., the astrophysicists and atomic physicists have little more in common than a common noun. Each represents a specialty, and dual comprehension in depth is simply humanly impossible.

In short, the classic paradox of the scholar—"The more you know, the more you know you do not know"—has no longer to wait for the humility of great wisdom to make itself evident. It is now an assumption, an initial premise. The question is no longer, "What do you think of creation?" Now we ask, "What is your specialization?" The result of such a world loss is frightening. We not only do not comprehend our world but also do not often comprehend those who could tell us about certain specialized aspects of it.

What is true for the natural sciences is likewise true for the social sciences and the humanities. The evidence in the natural sciences is more dramatic because of its mystifying and sophisticated use of signs, symbols, and numbers. But in point of fact, the knowledge explosion has produced a bewildering amount of nonscientific information, theories, and hypotheses which cannot be critically evaluated by one man in any one discipline, let alone all disciplines. The task of the biologist, the economist, and the artist can no longer be adequately represented and synthesized by the philosopher. Great comprehensive rational systems are historical relics of an earlier, more simplistic age.

The loss of comprehension tends to produce the very effects knowledge was to dispel—magic and superstitution. What man cannot understand, he tends to idolize or at least misuse. One needs only to look at contemporary advertising to find evidence of such magic: "This gasoline has K-7"; "This toothpaste has formula F24"; "This is one of the new 'miracle' drugs"; and "This detergent makes your automatic washer twenty feet tall." For our technologically intimidated brains, a formula, seemingly any formula, is the stamp of irrefutable excellence.

But the fragmentation of our world with its consequent idolization has more serious consequences than ritualized advertising. It also means that the control and restraint exercized by criticism and judgment are denied to any but the particular in-group. Thus politicians, academicians, clergy-men, *et al.* are told to refrain from trying to direct the military about which they have no expertise. Wars are controlled by military technicians, government is administered by political technicians, and souls are saved by theological technicians. Such a division of labor and jurisdiction of power produces a sense of helplessness and futility in the minds of most of us whose qualifications do not permit us to exercise judgment or control over the issues which determine the nature and destiny of our lives.

Another evident aspect of our world loss in the tech-nological age is the absence of standards, the loss of value. The old classic virtues of wisdom, justice, temperance, and

6   *The search for meaningful existence*

courage which seemed so reasonable to the Greeks, so natural to the Renaissance humanists, and so inevitable to the nineteenth-century moralists, have been discarded for the scientific interests of contemporary analytical philosophy and technology. The Freudian attack on the sovereignty of Reason and the scientific attack on the infallibility of Faith have shaken man's confidence in all value judgments but his own and in all moral standards but self-preservation. Technological man has come to the (perhaps sad) conclusion that he can detect no intrinsic value in the world or in men, that whatever value exists, exists only within the mind of the one who is evaluating. Consequently, the world becomes "my world, right or wrong," and there is no fear that such defiance will be penalized by some universal judgment or standard. When one, for economic, social, or political reasons is forced to act corporately, the same value void is in evidence. It simply now becomes "my family or firm or nation right or wrong," and again the implied standard of right and wrong carries no weight of pending judgment.

That such self-centered standards destroy community is evidenced everywhere: the indifference with which we view all tragedy but our own; our refusal to take stands on controversial issues for fear of social, economic, or political reprisals; our mistrust of our local and federal governments, which we politely call the "credibility gap"; the acknowledged price-fixing in some of our "blue-chip" corporations; American self-righteousness at Nuremburg and self-defensiveness in Vietnam. In all cases mistrust, disbelief, fear, and occasionally hatred result, and community is destroyed. While traditional values are given lip service, they receive recognition only when such values happen to coincide with our own.

Goodness, justice, honesty, honor are lost in a world totalized by technicians. Skill, efficiency, and indifference are valued but are not values. The result is a materialistic society directed by technically competent barbarians—one-dimensional, one-directional mass men who think in terms of quantification. In such a valueless society, there is no real despair for the simple reason that there is no real hope. Any ultimate ideal or transcendent orientation has been discarded as meaningless.

Life for the mass man, to put it briefly, is simple technique. To live is to develop the best technique possible: education is the technique for getting a job; a job is a technique for getting money; marriage is a technique of society organization and child-rearing; social adjustment is the technique of acceptance; sex is a relational technique; war and peace are military and political techniques. For the age of technical materialism, none of these things has any value in and of itself. It is the age which sees the tragedy of Willie Loman's life in Arthur Miller's *Death of a Salesman* to be that of a poor salesman in a tough district. The fact that he lacked what has traditionally been called "character" is completely inconsequential.

While it is true that this loss of relative standards can be accounted for by the prior loss of an ultimate standard, our age of technological affluence exposed such a loss by eliminating our self-righteous pretentiousness, by eliminating ostensible need. At one time our chief goal was to glorify God and to enjoy Him forever. By the turn of the century a subtle shift in orientation had taken place: now our chief end is to glorify life and to enjoy it for as long as possible.

Such a shift undoubtedly goes back to the theological optimism and liberalism of the nineteenth century. It is not difficult to justify an argument which advances the opinion that the finest way to glorify God is to provide abundantly for one's fellowmen. The trouble is that in our newly acquired technological ecstasy we ignored, and then forgot, our original altruistic motivation. Technology for its part did superbly well, so that for many Americans the greatest decision one has to face is whether one can afford Decor-Group #3 on his car this year and color television next year, or a second car (compact, of course) "for the wife and children."

When the age of affluence has eliminated universal need as a religious concern, the desperate poverty of materially oriented lives is exposed. One result of such exposure is the proliferation of small, fanatic, pseudoreligious value groups which try to fill the value vacuum, e.g., the K. K. K., Christian Anti-Communist Crusade, Hell's Angels, Black Panthers. Another reaction is withdrawal from what is considered to be a phony, purposeless society into some cultic detachment, if not isolation. The appearance of psychedelic communities with their injunction: "turn on, tune it, and drop out," is one of the more bizarre forms, the existence of Tolkien societies a gentler reaction.

For the many Americans who still belong to yet exploited minority groups, e.g., Negroes, Puerto Ricans, Indians, the problem of poverty and prejudice has, unfortunately, only retarded the recognition of this loss of value. Deprived of the affluence of "white America," equality, dignity, and even freedom are usually defined in materialistic terms. This creates a double problem, for as these groups do attain—often through great sacrifice and suffering—the desperately needed goods and services, they, like the white majority earlier, are finding that such affluence has little to do with equality, dignity, and freedom. As a result, such groups have the double disillusionment of having sacrificed and fought for a partially phony prize and of having lost what was the most important thing of all—the rationale for genuine integration into a new and enlightened establishment. Is it any wonder such frustration expresses itself in the multi-inflammatory phrase of the Watts riot in California— "Burn, baby, burn!"

The affluence of our technological society has shown us the poverty of our standardless life. Value, for its own sake or for God's sake, seems no longer plausible, and value for my sake becomes so relative that it lacks any relevance. Therefore it is not surprising to see a great interest in the recent emergence of situational and consensus ethics. Situation ethics begins with an analysis of my position relative to the balance of forces (mine and those imposed upon me) involved in any given situation. Moral sanction and approval are then given to those calculated actions of mine which are in keeping with such possibilities and prohibitions. Consensus ethics begins with an analysis of pertinent opinion concerning a given ethical problem and its probable solution. Here moral sanction and approval are given to those calculated actions of mine which confirm such a consensus. The value, in each case, is determined by the skill with which I analyze the situation and act; the value is not determined by the quality of my act itself. In other words, responsibility is understood in terms of data accuracy; value is equated with my personal data processing and not with my act of moral (i.e., value) decision. In the end we are really no better off with or without such ethical techniques, for my action is the result of *my* interpretation and *my* evaluation for *my* benefit. The posture is still defensive and egocentric.

Another characteristic of our contemporary life which has driven us into the search for the New Humanism is the loss of eventfulness. That is, things happen—men come and go, laws come and go, governments rise and fall, wars begin and sometimes end—but nothing significant really seems to occur. No changes in man's life, no changes in his relationship to his fellow man, no innovations in his world are noted or celebrated, so that one can say with conviction, "This is new! This is noteworthy!" Only the names, times, and numbers change: Hitlers become Stalins, become Maos, become Hos; Germany becomes Korea, becomes the Middle East, becomes Vietnam; the Republican Platform becomes the Democratic Platform, becomes the Republican Platform, etc., etc., etc. Endless variations on a single theme is the only variety there is. It is Samuel Beckett's Godot-world of Vladimir and Estragon in which "Nothing happens, nobody comes, nobody goes, it's awful."

Rather than leading to any certainty or fixity, such loss of eventfulness leads only to immobility. With nothing to be accomplished, motivation is deprived of its power and direction. Tradition becomes an empty word, or at best a synonym of repetition. History is reduced to past happening which, in an eventless and absurd world, offers neither insight into the present nor wisdom for the future.

This eventless existence is the chosen world of many young student radicals, those who would trust no one over thirty years of age. Were history genuinely eventful, so that there would be an extension of causal and meaningful relationship, then one would be tied to, formed by, or even obligated to that history and to the future for which one would be the responsible agent. But in the name of freedom, the New Radicals disavow any such obligation to the past. There is, for them, no necessary correlation between objective historical happenings and subjective eventfulness experienced in terms of an immediate encounter with others. When tradition gets in the way, one ignores it. The only meaning is *now*. Prediction is passé.

The sociologist Paul Goodman makes a similar observation about the New Radicals' rejection of the relevance of history: "When the young today look back to the Bible, John Locke, and Immanuel Kant, they cannot realize that all this was for real. They will have to make their own way. The loss of tradition is tragic because a generation cannot break away from a past into bold new creative patterns if it has no relationship to the past."[1]

What is behind such an attitude of historical indifference? Why, for this generation of young adults, has history lost its meaning? I doubt if most of them would be able to provide the reason. As a matter of fact, they would probably suggest that the wrong questions were being asked, that the burden of proof belongs on those who claim that history is meaningful. It is a rejection in terms of negation; history is eventless, meaningless because it was never eventful and meaningful. One cannot lose what one has never possessed.

Behind such an assertion of negation is the understanding that eventfulness is comprised of more than "happenings," that an event means alteration or change which carries with it, at least to some degree, the characteristic of irrevocability. For a happening to be an event means that it must demonstrate its integration within a meaningful sequence of happenings. The sequence of happenings apparent to this young generation can be described only chronologically—as occurrences antecedent to or subsequent to a given, identifiable happening. However, in terms of meaning and the sense of irrevocability, the apparent and experienced sequence is absurd.

For meaning to be established and the sequence of occurrences to be eventful, there must be a point beyond history, a transcendent reference, which enables the observer to make such an affirmation. This is the force of Nietzsche's observation in *The Joyful Wisdom*, the *locus classicus* of the death-of-God theologians.

"Where is God gone," he (the Madman) called out. "I mean to tell you! *We have killed him,*—you and I! We are all his murderers! But how have we done it? How were we able to drink up the sea? Who gave us the sponge to wipe away the whole horizon? What did we do when we loosened the earth from its sun? Whither does it now move? Whither do we move? Away from all suns? Do we not dash on increasingly? Backwards, sideways, forewards, in all directions? Is there still an above and below? Do we not stray as through an infinite nothingness?"[2]

If there is no point of reference, no end, no beginning, then process is reduced to sequence.

The disenchantment of such an insight was dulled for one hundred years by the incredible fulfillment of the technological promise of Things; but, as in the case of the loss of values, Things cannot provide a substitute for eventless, purposeless existence. Once basic physical needs are met by a seemingly assured affluence, boredom begins. Boredom begets indolence or fanaticism, withdrawal or revolt. The argument that our affluence does not touch four-fifths of the world where poverty and need still exist does not touch the hearts of a people become defensive because of the absurdity of history. It is every man for himself, every country for itself; there is no judgment, there is only success or failure here and now. There is not much of Ferlinghetti's "wonder" in the loss of eventfulness.

A fourth characteristic of our technological age which prompts our search for the New Humanism is the loss of meaning. In one sense this loss has been evident in the loss of continuity, value, and eventfulness. Each of these aspects of life involves meaning, e.g., coherence, structure, purpose, and relevance. But at the heart of meaning comes identity, personal identity, and understanding of who *I* am. It is I who create or perceive meaning in my world; and meaning, in this fundamental sense, can be understood as the acknowledged correlation between myself and the world.

The character of such meaning thus depends principally upon the nature of my identity, but it is just this—my identity —which has been called into question. In this technological age to say that I am a child of God is to talk incomprehensibly. Even should I like the sentiment, I don't know what the words "child of God" really mean. The theistic orientation which traditionally gave man his identity and determined his relationship to the world because it identified his God, has ceased to be effective or necessary in the one-dimensional world of the technological man. His mental and physical health and his social well-being are all included in his programmed technical coverage. His identity is no longer symbolized by the receiving of a personal name marking his unique relation to God but is rather marked by the receiving of a social security number which is the symbol of his interaction with his society. He is no longer the recipient of a *vocatio*, a calling, but rather "has" a vocation, "gets a job." His identity, in the technological age, is equated with his function: man is a doctor, lawyer, or restaurant chef.

While such an identification seemed to have the advantage of releasing man from a burdensome, obscure, and—at times—inhuman obligation to some transcendent authority who required a personal response, it has had the decided disadvantage of encouraging depersonalized, functional relationships in which contemporary technological man finds himself expendable. Lawrence, Jonathan, and Allen as personalities cannot be replaced, but doctors, lawyers, and restaurant chefs can. In the technological age no man's personality is indispensable, only his function may be. It is a shattering blow to lose one's identity, to be missed but not remembered.

But what of man's interaction with his society? Is not his identity, lost in functionalism, regained in human interaction? This would seem to be the suggestion of such social psychologists as Harry Stack Sullivan and George Herbert Mead. According to the social psychologist man learns about himself as a self in his contact with other selves. I am informed about who I am by observing the reaction of others to me and my reaction to them. The identity of self, then, is provided by this dual action of the self which sees, and sees itself as seen by others. In short, personality and identity, according to these scholars, are social constructs.

Yet it is just such a process of social identity which, in the technological age, seems to deprive man of his individuality and thereby his identity. Our lack of authenticity, our loss of true humanism, our loss of spiritual identity mark all aspects of culture. The System, the Organization, necessitated by the complicated and mutually dependent specializations of this automated age, may not be the reason for this loss of identity, but it is at least the partial occasion of its occurrence. Such an observation has led Russell Baker to suggest facetiously that the pledge of allegiance be rewritten for the twentieth-century American: " 'I pledge allegiance to the computer and to the machine for which it stands, one organization, under I.B.M., inescapable, with punch cards and dossiers on all.' "[3]

On the verge of everyman's Eden because of our affluence, it may be that what we will achieve is not paradise but purgatory—that the Great Society now envisaged is more of a threat than a treasure, that mass society means the emergence of a mass man, exposed through mass media to mass taste made available because of mass production. Such total exposure to mediocrity and total availability of consumer goods can prove to be stifling to any imaginative or creative life. If the social psychologist is right, then mass man structures his life within a mass culture and economy which militate against not only values but also any form or idea of individuality. As earlier, when identity was considered in terms of function, so again the resulting depersonalization of man's identity convinces him that he is expendable, or that at least a reasonable facsimile of him is available at an increasing cut-rate.

Mass culture mutilates meaning. It produces a nonvalue

society marked, as Mr. Jack Newfield suggests, by "hypocrisy called Brotherhood Week; assembly lines called colleges; conformity called status; bad taste called Camp; and quiet desperation called success."[4] The awesome fact which begins to emerge is the continuous growth and seeming inevitability of such structure. As more and more people mass the earth[5] (an estimated 15 billion by the year 2000), the necessity of conformity mounts, so that even a protest against conformity necessarily employs the very system it seeks to destroy. The hope for identity with any degree of personal uniqueness seems to be fading rather than brightening, and this is the mark of our loss of meaning, our loss of spiritual identity.

To exist as a human being is to have something to live for, i.e., it is to be ultimately concerned about the *meaning* of one's existence. It is to ask the question which only I can ask, "Why *my* existence?" Yet this, asked out of my total involvement with my world, is not a psychological question nor a sociological question; it is a religious question asked not speculatively, but out of the depth of existential concern and involvement. Any other orientation is superficial. In an age when the traditional religious questions are dismissed as irrelevant and the sociological formula is inadequate and inappropriate, the unanswered question of identity only emphasizes the loss of meaning. Arthur Miller's lawyer, Quentin, in *After the Fall* well understands this loss of identity and meaning:

You know . . . more and more I think that for many years I looked at life like a case at law, a series of proofs. When you're young, you prove how brave you are, or smart; then, what a good lover; then good father; finally, how wise, or powerful or what-the-hell-ever. But underlying it all, I see now, there was a presumption. That I was moving on an upward path toward some elevation, where—God knows what . . .—I would be justified, or even condemned . . . a *verdict* anyway. I think now that my disaster really began when I looked up one day—and the bench was empty. No judge in sight. And all that remained was the endless argument with oneself—this pointless litigation of existence before an empty bench. Which, of course, is another way of saying despair. And, of course, despair can be a way of life; but you have to believe in it, pick it up, take it to heart, and move on again. Instead, I seem to be caught; hung up waiting for some believable sign. And the days and the months and now the years are drawing away.[6]

Such thoughts, such emptiness, and such world loss have driven our society in at least three directions—towards a self-centered, technological amoralism, towards an Eastern mysticism, and into the search for a New Humanism. The first of these alternatives is defensive and self-destructive; the second anticommunal and escapist; the third, alone, holds open the possibility for the reassertion of a humanistic and therefore meaningful historical continuity. It is therefore with this alternative that the following essay is concerned.

The word "new" is used in the phrase "New Humanism" because the transition from nineteenth-century Victorianism into twentieth-century technocentrism has been marked by extraordinary artistic, philosophical, and theological activity and by the so-called social and moral revolutions, e.g., the "Rock Revolution," the "Sex Revolution," the "Educational Revolution." But such terminology is perhaps too journalistic, too grand for what is really occurring. What have been labeled "revolutions" are actually loosely structured rebellions, expressions of dissatisfaction with an rejection of superficial, hypocritical, or inadequate norms of the Culture Establishment. In place of such norms new expressions of meaning, new forms, new techniques, new attempts to express reality in terms of authenticity, freedom, and affirmation, and hints of a new morality have emerged. Contemporary man is involved in a dramatic humanistic venture. He is trying to see himself from a new perspective, and it is the purpose of this essay to help clarify the image.

Clearly, then, the search for the New Humanism is not confined to the private domain of professional philosophers and theologians or to the public demonstrations of university students. It has become the *cause célebre* of men representing the whole of our society. It is with the more unconventional, more artistic forms of the search that I should like to begin this essay. The criticisms and insights, the rebellion and reconstruction offered by these protesting artists and scholars are surely as valid as those of the professional value seekers. All are searching for a rebirth of wonder; all would seem to be telling the Age of Anxiety to drop dead.

two: *The revolt*

THE MOST WIDELY publicized (but not the earliest) form of rebellion against the dehumanization of the technological society was the Free Speech Movement on the campus of the University of California at Berkeley. But now we are "Beyond Berkeley"—or so we are being told. The Free Speech Movement has lost its charismatic charter; Mario Savio, the not-so-charismatic student leader was left knocking at a door he once could have opened by himself; and the Berkeley Radicals have ostensibly gone back to the primary task of getting an education.

More recently, at a Washington, D.C., protest march against American policy in Vietnam, the student Radicals from around the country found themselves delivered by the experienced old hands of Dr. Benjamin Spock into (what must seem to them) the everlasting arms of Norman Thomas, all under the maternal eye of Mrs. Martin Luther King. For some critical observers this must seem like poetic justice for a movement which began by stating: "We trust no one over thirty," and then, under pressure of justification, stated even more categorically: "Now we don't trust anyone at all."

What has happened to the great revolt? Does the decline of university demonstrations, their loss of power, and lack of leadership—Staughton Lynd, Paul Potter, Joan Baez, and Bob Dylan notwithstanding—mean that Berkeley was, as many hoped, merely the symbol of student frustration at the impersonality of the multiversity? Such a conclusion would seem to support the contention that the problem of revolt and estrangement has been overstated; that the problem is technical rather than moral or spiritual; that the problem can be, and in part has been, solved by establishing self-contained colleges within the university, by introducing new curricula, and by improving the university's "internal" public relations and counseling services. But such a technical, methodological analysis of the problem is all too simple. "To define misery and discontent," to quote Professor Edgar Friedenberg, "primarily as a problem of adjustment is one of the oldest ploys used by our society to disarm the troublemakers among its young. In fact, we have so powerfully institutionalized this defense against recognizing that students might have something valid and realistic to complain about that we can no longer escape it even when we want to."[1]

Perhaps a key to an understanding of the revolt of the student Radicals is to be found in its lack of form, its lack of focus, its lack of leadership, its lack of organization, and its persistent lack of articulation. Most of us expect a revolution to be going somewhere, to have a goal or gospel—yet here we apparently have those who think of themselves as "rebels without a cause." It is, as Jack Newfield terms it, a "Revolt without Dogma." This is not to imply that the rebels are intellectually incompetent or emotionally childish. They are, in fact, cautious, thoughtful eclectics. These rebels, despite a fringe-group flirtation with Communism, are far more inclined to read Albert Camus than Karl Marx. As political protesters, they listen to Professor Staughton Lynd far more willingly than to Lyndon Johnson. As strong advocates of civil rights, the student Radicals give their allegiance to a variety of *ad hoc* student groups rather than to SCLC, NAACP, or CORE. Even Saul Alinsky reportedly merits cautious respect from the students, though they do no fully approve his autocratic ways.

What meaning can we find in this seemingly meaningless collage? I think it becomes apparent that the student Radicals, the so-called activists, are not out to change the world as they democratically desire it to be, but only as they *know* it to have become. These new Radicals are not out to overthrow democracy but to achieve it; they are not out to change civil rights but to implement them, to make them consistent with human rights; they are not out to change higher education but to become truly educated. What they desire, they state, is not their own way but a way of their own.

For these Radicals, the villain, in every case, is the Structure, the System, the Regulation, the Establishment, which prevents one from experiencing the full life, an authentic life. It is the Establishment which includes the Multiversity, Big Business, Big Labor, Big Government, the Military, and even Big Church, which prevents any genuine, human self-realization and any meaningful commitment. To become a part of such a system is to become a participant in its crimes. To act meaningfully is to act personally in such a way as to draw maximum attention to the injustice of impersonal society. The System is the agent of depersonalization, the landlord for Harrington's "Other America."

Now, perhaps, we can see why such disorganization exists in the radical movement. They read Camus rather than Marx, for Camus is not doctrinaire; he tries, rather, to bring some human warmth and dignity into an absurd world, where wars maim men and diseases cripple children. The Radicals listen to Staughton Lynd, because he talks in terms of justice and human suffering, rather than in terms of justification and world-police power. These Radicals follow *ad hoc* civil rights groups because their structure (if they have one) is never obtrusive, never claims priority over their mission or action, which begins with the people at the shack-slum level. However should their organization or character change, the students would abandon them as quickly as they once adopted them.

In short, the student Radicals believe that the Establishment has failed to translate educational, political, and social ideals into realities. Even the liberals have betrayed fundamental human values in the name of compromise and accommodation. In the 1962 Port Huron Statement of the Students for a Democratic Society (SDS), which is the most definitive position paper the New Radicals have, this declaration occurs: "We oppose the depersonalization that reduces human beings to the status of things—if anything, the brutalities of the twentieth century teach that means and ends are intimately related, that vague appeals to 'posterity' cannot justify present mutilations." Indicative of this attitude was the fact that one Vietnam war protest, initiated at Haverford but observed by colleges across the country, was a fast. In talking with some of the students who participated, I had the impression that they were not trying seriously to force a discussion of issues or principles on the government or their fellow students. Rather, they were attempting, for a brief number of hours, to disassociate themselves from an absurd impersonal world and to identify themselves with those who suffer from its dehumanizing structure and power.

General student response to the dilemma, however, either tends toward an unambiguous activism which makes a contribution toward "communitarian democracy" by moving outside Establishment politics, or tends to try to escape the dilemma by actively disavowing its respect for, or its responsibility to, Establishment value norms. The first group has been called the Concerned Generation, the New Realists, the New Democrats, as well as the New Radicals. These titles are indicative of the fact that the point of departure is a radical humanism. The activities of these students are indicative of their seriousness. Many such *ad hoc* humanist groups are citizenship councils which initiate remedial and adult education programs based on the belief that college students need to be involved in the world beyond the campus and that students do have talents and abilities which can be put to good use in their communities. In this same spirit students across the country have been involved in education endeavors from Operation Head Start to "senior citizens" projects. The Peace Corps, the Northern Student Movement, Students for a Democratic Society, all have sought to bring into society some sense of personal dignity, respect, meaning, and love. On the nature of man, the Port Huron Statement makes this affirmation: "We regard man as infinitely precious and possessed of unfulfilled capacities for reason, freedom, and love."

With the other groups of students who are endeavoring primarily to escape, the use of transfer, alcohol, pot, drugs, sex, and even suicide is symptomatic of the same revolt against meaningless conformity and structure. The transfer to another campus is tried because the student temporarily can equate novelty and variation with self-transformation; alcohol and drugs are used because they seem, at least for a moment, to lift one beyond the reality of the stereotyping society, giving the students, say our medical authorities, the illusion of being close to one another, of being someone in an expendable world. Sex is the same experience. The appeal of free love is that it is open and honest. To confine sex to marriage, they say, is to confine it to Structure, to the System, which is to admit that the Structure is supreme even in the most intimate and responsible of human relations. Suicide speaks for itself. It is the tragic and final admission to oneself and to the world that one can't beat the System and that with the System there is no meaning. Of course all of these symbols are at times abused; not all of these students are engaged in an honest search for identity. But, one cannot discount honest exploration because of some exploitation anymore than one can discredit truth because of lies.

The most indigenous expression, and for many observers the most promising expression, of student reaction to the irrelevance, impersonality, and technical functionalism of American higher education is the establishment of "free" universities across the country—in New York, Detroit, Chicago, Austin, San Francisco, *et al.* These self-styled universities are "free" not in the monetary sense but "free" in the presuppositions governing academic inquiry. The complaint voiced by the faculty and students of these universities is that conventional colleges and universities with their historical obligations, irrelevant requirements, academic vested-interests, and subservience to the Establishment dollar are no longer capable or qualified to speak to the contemporary world. Hope for intellectual honesty is not possible in simple reform, but only in rebirth.

The movement, which originally had strong political ties to the left and encouraged a kind of cultural bohemianism, has since broadened its impact and ignored its infant orientation. With the rebellion against regimentation came, also, the constructive and affirmative experience of the Freedom Schools of Mississippi and the Ghetto Schools of the North. Education, wherever it is found, must be relevant to the times, free to explore and probe these contemporary problems in context, and open to the creative insights and abilities of its participants.

Some universities and colleges, which obviously do not feel threatened by such a movement, have actually invited the "free" university to establish itself within the institution and to utilize its facilities. This is not an effort to tame or to smother such free expression; it is the recognition that the university may profit greatly from breakthroughs in curricula and methodology provided by such experimentation. This arrangement also provides the added benefit of unintimidated participation on the part of regular faculty members, many of whom are sympathetic to the cause. In these instances, the movement toward meaning is an act of the whole academic community rather than the disruptive and divisive act of a few.

By this time there may be enough justification for an important point that should be made: that the protest, the revolution if you will, taking place on campuses across the nation is not an isolated, academic affair. The revolt spills over into our cultural, political, and spiritual life. What has been examined thus far is simply the recent academic syndrome of a protest of much wider scope. The fact that academe has received such attention is due, in part, to the improvident handling and consequent publicity of the Berkeley demonstration.

As the students are involved, so are many men involved in the search for a New Morality. Our lack of authenticity, our loss of spiritual identity, in short, our lack of a true humanism, mark all aspects of culture. The Structure, the Establishment, the System—if not the source of evil—is at least the partial occasion of its expression; and it is well for us to see this and see it clearly, lest we, concentrating on the students' rebellion, find only the apple and miss the snake.

Corroboration for such a hypothesis comes from our artists, philosophers, and theologians. Representatives of the latter two groups will be considered in the next chapter. For the present let us look at the contributions of those who are considered by many to be the true prophets of any age, the artists. "We are brought back," writes Stephen Spender, "to the necessity of art because the arts of imagination which are poetry, music, painting, result from the immediate experiencing by means of the artist's senses, the whole of his being, of the circumstances of a time and a place. Art expresses the truth that despite all our systems of knowledge and analysis, to grasp, to get the feeling of our world, we are driven back on to ourselves, our own feelings."[2] Of the three forms which Stephen Spender cites, painting, as representative of the graphic arts, is an appropriate place to begin. None of the other arts has had more exposure, ridicule, lionization, and analysis than this form, which perhaps is indicative of its power to "reach" us, to move and influence us.

Of course, in such a short look at art, many forms, many prominent artists, and many popular movements must necessarily be excluded. In fact, it would be only fair to point out that the great majority of artists simply "paint" or "create" and do not attempt to articulate or explain *why* they create or what it *means*; this would not occur to them as necessary or germane, any more than explaining jazz seems necessary to Louis Armstrong. If the art is pure—painting or jazz—it defies translation, and if one needs translation, then comprehension is already precluded. Nevertheless, commentary in any art helps, and where possible, comments and explanations by major artists have been included. The major movements which structure our times are discussed, and many representative artists are simply silent witnesses to the power of the revolt which has liberated Western art from its confinement to Western tradition. Because the New Humanism which is being sought is not simply the traditional humanism of rational values but is a humanism involving the whole man, it should express itself effectively and convincingly within such art mediums as painting or music or literature, i.e., on their own terms and with their own terminology. The denotation of philosophical or theological language can, at times, distort truth which is revealed in the ambiguities of art.

Our first encounter with avant-garde art usually leaves us wondering whether the artist is "pulling our leg" or simply lives in a world totally unrelated to ours. This second impression is likely to have more validity than the first. However, the artist is convinced that the alienation which we attribute to him is really indicative of our own.

Never, with the possible exception of the Roman Empire, has so large a part of the best artistic creation been bitter, despairing, contemptuous, and destructive. With rare exceptions, the works most, and most justly, admired by intellectuals are counsels of despair. We produce parodies, denunciations, and nightmares. On the whole, our best artists are engaged in disrupting patterns, smashing forms, and deliberately cultivating dissonances in painting and music, as well as in poetry, fiction, and drama. They engage in no promising dialogue with either the statesman, the scientist, or the majority of their fellow citizens. They have, in their own way, signed off from their civilization almost as effectively as has the cultivated manufacturer of the shapeless dream.[3]

The contemporary artists believes that most of us live in an artificial world of technological systems which produce a stultifying conformity to meaningless cultural norms. Therefore, convinced that traditional Formalism, Stylization, and System severely limit if not preclude much which he has to express of himself and of his perception of the world, the contemporary artist began his search for freedom, authenticity, and meaning.

Four artists at the turn of the twentieth century can be considered the major precursors of our contemporary movements: Cézanne, Gauguin, VanGogh, and Munch. Paul

Cézanne is often called the father of modern art, for it was he who first successfully broke free from the rigid limits of traditionalism, from artifically "composed" landscapes and academic conventions. He had no hesitation in using distortion deliberately to achieve desired effects. It was Cézanne's experimentation which led to the development of Cubism in the work of Picasso and Braque. Paul Gauguin found release from the sterility of Western formalism in the exotic primitivism of the South Pacific. In Gauguin's famous painting "Where do we come from? What are we? Where are we going?" one cannot make the usual distinctions between the intellectual and sensuous elements. Its sensitivity of expression is part of its religious quest for reality. The vitality of reality involves new forms of expression, a new use of color. This new dynamism is also evident in the painting of Vincent VanGogh. In terms of his own personal symbolism, VanGogh paints his subjective involvement, even identification, with the world. His stylistic violence simply destroys what to that time had been accepted form and confronts the viewer in an existential way with his own identity. The Norwegian painter Edward Munch, perhaps even more dramatically than Van-Gogh, gave expression to the power and prominence of man's emotional and psychic life, the tensions and anxieties of which man is existentially aware. See, for example, Munch's lithographs "The Cry" and "Anxiety." His demand is for sanity in terms of self-understanding not societal norms, for expression in terms of humanism not propriety.

It was primarily the influence of these four men in revolt against the naturalistic representations of Impressionism, the culmination of Western realism in painting, which led to the development of the two traditions which dominate contemporary art—Expressionism and Dadaism. It is in these two movements that conscious revolt against the meaninglessness of sheer formalism appears. Dadaism, though a decade younger than Expressionism, is the more defiant and negative revolt form and should be considered first. The meaningless name "Dada" itself is indicative of the attitude of the group of young painters who founded the movement in Zurich, Switzerland, in 1916. It is an audacious assertion of the irrational in the face of sweet reason. Marcel Duchamp, who painted the much discussed, much criticized "Nude Descending a Staircase," states that Dadaism is "a metaphysical attitude—a sort of nihilism . . . a way to get out of a state of mind—to avoid being influenced by one's immediate environment, or by the past; to get away from cliches—to get free."[4] The Dada revolt is not simply destructive therefore, but it is an attempt to avoid the stultifying superficialities induced by formal patterns. However, one of the most recent expressions of Dadaism, Pop art—the exploitation of the banalities of cultural commercialism and chauvinism, Andy Warhol's soup cans, et al.—tends to be a decadent, maybe "comic" vestige of a once serious revolt against the tyranny of traditional forms. Roy Lichtenstein, one of the best of the Pop artists, believes that Pop art is antiexperimental; it is also "anti-contemplative, anti-nuance, anti-getting-away-from-the-tyranny-of-the-rectangle, anti-movement-and-light, anti-mystery, anti-paint-quality, anti-zen, and anti all those brilliant ideas of preceding movements which everyone understands so thoroughly."[5] Pop art accepts the world on its own terms, for what it appears to be. Consequently it makes no value judgments, good or bad, nor moral judgments, good or evil; it simply reflects the world as the world wants to see itself. Any judgment must come from the viewer. Any attempt at coping with the predicament of mass culture other than the presentation of its colossal banality is also absent. Robert Indiana believes that, "Art, Pop or otherwise, hardly provides the Solution—some optimistic, glowing, harmonious, humanitarian, plastically perfect Lost Chord of Life."[6] Pop art, in any case, does not add much beyond protest to the search for the New Humanism.

The major movement of artistic revolt is Expressionism. It is from the impetus and influence of this movement that most of our avant-garde art comes. At the risk of oversimplification, one can point to the formation of "Der Blaue Reiter" group in Germany in 1911 by Wassily Kandinsky and Franz Marc as the beginning of the Expressionist movement. Opposed to Impressionism's concern for external reality, Expressionism is concerned with internal vision. The relationship between the artist and his world, understood in terms of a personal, emotional, even spiritual response, is of central importance. Marc wrote:

Art is metaphysical . . . it will free itself from man's purposes and desires. We will no longer paint the forest or the horse as they please us or appear to us, but as they really are, as the forest or the horse feel themselves—their absolute being—which lives behind the appearances which we see. We will be successful in so far as we can succeed in overcoming the traditional "logic" of millennia with artistic creativity. There are art forms which are abstract, which can never be proven by human knowledge. These forms have always existed, but were always obscured by human knowledge and desire. The faith in art itself was lacking, but we shall build it: it lives on the "other side."[7]

It would be difficult to find a more explicit statement of the correlation which exists between the artistic and philosophical revolt against traditional Western (Greek) idealism. It might initially sound as though Marc were actually supporting idealism with his mention of a horse's "absolute being—which lives behind the appearances." Such language does raise the specter of Platonic dualism, of appearance and reality. But Marc risks such language for two reasons: to make clear the distinction which exists between his intent and the intent of the earlier Impressionists; and to express his concern for the total reality of this particular horse, not simply his own visual impression of it. What both he and Kandinsky sought was a unified, organic effect involving color, style, and form, i.e., a new concept of content. "Is there a more mysterious idea for the artist," writes Marc, "than the conception of how nature may be mirrored in the eye of the animal? . . . How poor and how souless is our convention of placing animals in a landscape which belongs to our eyes, instead of penetrating into the soul of the animal in order to imagine his perception."[8] If one views Marc's paintings "The Tower of the Blue Horses," "Red Horses," or "Horse in Landscape," one can sense the attempt, in terms of both color and form, to capture this new concept of content.

Mention should be made of two other painters of the period who believed that they could achieve an expression of reality only if they abandoned traditional formalism for the informalism of a primitive spontaneity. August Marke, a member of "Der Blaue Reiter" group, wrote in an essay entitled "The Masks:" "To create form means to live. Are not the children who construct directly from the secrets of their emotions more creative than the imitators of Greek form? Are not the savages artists, who have their own form, strong as the form of thunder?"[9] Marke's painting "Storm" with all its expressive primitive violence is an excellent example of his thought. The other painter is Henri Rousseau, a self-taught French artist, whose finest work is a naive primitivism peopled by Eden-like innocents, animals, and lush vegetation. Kandinsky called his work the "great realism" even though (or maybe because) Rousseau's sources of inspiration were his dreams and his imagination. Though not a member of "Der Blaue Reiter" group, his work was of great influence within it. Franz Marc wrote to the artist Robert Delaunay: "The douanier Rousseau is the only one whose art often haunts me. I constantly attempt to understand how he painted his marvelous pictures. I try to identify myself with the inner state of this venerable painter, that is to say, with a state of great love."[10]

Of course the constant danger of such an artistic revolt is pure subjectivism in which *I* simply substitute *my* purpose or *my* perception for another's isolated claim, which would be no metaphysical revolt after all but simply another form of Greek idealism. In the later development of Abstract Expressionism, in representative paintings of such artists as Picasso, Miro, Mondrian, Klee, and Pollock this subjectivism was often evident. The possibility of this development was evident to Kandinsky early in the movement. Kandinsky predicted that the final predominance of the abstract would be inevitable. He said that the choice of subjects must originate from the inner necessity of the artist, and that material, or objective, form might be more or less superfluous. He insisted that the artist must be given complete freedom to express himself according to the "principle of inner necessity." He looked hopefully to the future: "When the possibility of speaking through artistic means will be developed, it will become superfluous to borrow from the exterior world for spiritual expression."[11]

Much of modern and contemporary art has not gone to this subjective expressionist extreme, and there is real evidence in the representational painting of such artists as VanGogh, Rouault, Picasso, Orozco, Shahn, Wyeth, Lebrun, and Baskin that points to the emergence of a new conscious expression of humanism. Seldon Rodman observes that, "a growing number of artists . . . are creating an art of total commitment—and in the grand manner, as artists like them always have. But the fact that they are creating an art about man and for man does not imply that men are prepared to accept it"[12]—one might add here, parenthetically, "or prepared to understand it." Paul Klee, for example, ends his essay *On Modern Art* with the plea "But we seek a people." Despite such evident lack of preparation on the part of the public, these artists, searching to express a new humanism, believe that it is their obligation to paint and to proclaim. Jose Orozco, the Mexican artist, addressing the social upheaval in his own country at the time of the Mexican Revolution, really includes all humanity when he writes to a friend:

What matters is boldness in thinking with a high-pitched voice; in speaking out about things as one feels them in the moment of speaking; in having the temerity to proclaim what one believes to be true without fear of consequences. . . . If one were to await the possession of the absolute truth, one must be either a fool or a mute. If the creative impulse were muted, the world would then be stayed on its march.[13]

Orozco's comments also bring to focus one of the artists' most cherished conditions for life—freedom. By freedom the artist does not mean simply the absence of political or physical restraint, important as this is he also means freedom in self-expression, in creation, freedom from the necessity to conform to rule or tradition. It is freedom in this latter form which interests Paul Klee and the Expressionists, freedom "which does not lead to fixed phases of development, representing exactly what nature one was, or will be, or could be on another star. But . . . freedom which merely demands its rights, the right to develop. . . ."[14] The revolt in art has genuinely freed the artist from tradition and for tradition— everything and anything are available for his creative use. Freedom is thus the ground of the creative act, its possibility and its limitation. Creation is *now* and therefore always incomplete. Genesis, believes Klee, is eternal.

While it is much easier to see and understand the contributions of representational art—that which employs recognizable forms and figures in its subject matter—nonrepresentational art, e.g., Abstract Expressionism, also makes its contribution toward the search for a New Humanism, even if it does so by graphically exposing the meaninglessness of a world technologically defined and described. George Biddle in *The Yes and No of Contemporary Art* states:

. . . Although the extreme Expressionism of the hour is in no sense an organic element of the Modern Movement—of the search for a new faith—yet it does express the uncertainty, the hopelessness, the moral despair of a tortured world which has drifted from its mooring and found no anchorage to which it can cling. In this sense, it is the negative, defeated, backward looking protest of contemporary art. . . .[15]

It would seem to me that we can credit Abstract Expressionism with more contribution than sheer negation. Non-representational art, by the very fact of its lack of traditional forms, its jarring juxtapositions of color, its abuse of traditional perspectives, and the absence of recognizable contexts or patterns, actually performs the function of freeing us for an awareness of life (or for an "aesthetic experience") which would be impossible through traditional representational paintings. Such Expressionism focuses our attention here and now, not on the prefigured, anticipated, or remembered. It represents what Georges Mathieu means by stating that in Abstract Expressionism the sign precedes its signification. Very often what is directly addressed by such painting is the subconscious.

The contemporary artist shocks us into life by (often) outrageous artistic expressions which he calls serious and the average layman thinks ridiculous, even scandalous. The layman looks at Paul Klee's "The Mocker Mocked" and wonders about the identity of the Mocker. But the contemporary artist is, above all things, a humanist—not in the classical sense of the possessor of specific traits and virtues, but in the contemporary sense of commitment, the inclusive involvement of the total man. Art, for such men, is not aesthetics but faith; it is the ultimate concern about which the existentialists speak. Realism and abstraction are not metaphysical opposites nor ends in themselves but means by which the artist can give full expression to such concern. The artist Robert Motherwell in a letter to Frank O'Hara dated August 18, 1965, writes: "The ultimate act is faith, the ultimate resource the preconscious: if either is suspended, the artist is impotent. This is possible any hour any day, and it is the artist's nightmare throughout life."[16] For Robert Motherwell it is not society to which he is responsive, but humanity.

The search for new meaning in terms of new expression, technique, and method is as clearly evident in music as it is in art, and the same limitations of this study apply. Only critical movements are mentioned and only a few musicians are quoted. Most composers are busy simply writing music, not philosophical tracts. Yet within the idiom of music itself, it is possible to see expressions of the New Humanism emerging in terms of freedom and integrity of composition. In so far as music is expressive of the composer himself and is written for our involvement, it is part of contemporary humanism.

The search begins with a reaction movement against German Romanticism of the nineteenth century. The German Romantic tradition culminated in the rich emotional (if sometimes strained) grandeur of Richard Wagner's music. His compositions were characterized by continuous melody, heavy and opulent orchestration, and "leitmotifs" which gave his music a highly personal and subjective character. The revolt against the excesses of the Romantic movement came, as in art, with the Impressionists.

The Impressionists wanted to return to the reality of the "objective" world and to curb the overindulgence of the

Romantics' emotional and personalized tone portraits. The break away from German art-music began mid-nineteenth century with the Russian composer Michael Glinka who used national folk music as the basis of his compositions. Such a break heralded not only the rise of Nationalism in Western music but also the abandonment of many of the traditional Western forms, e.g., sonatas, fugues, and development sections. Glinka was followed by a composer of even greater stature, Modeste Mussorgsky whose opera *Boris Godunov*, with its effort to be natural, direct, and real, set the stage for the great Western Impressionist Claude Debussy.

Impressionism in music, as in art, is not as much the first act of the revolutionary drama as it is the last act of Western formalism. But, just because Impressionism is a reaction movement against the excesses of Romanticism, it does produce some innovations which become transitional for the twentieth-century revolt. In endeavoring to dramatize the objective world as it is, the Impressionist has introduced new rhythms and has exercised a new freedom in harmonic expression. Debussy, influenced by the poetry of Mallarmé and the painting of Edouard Manet as well as by composers such as Mussorgsky, began to use new chords and combinations of chords in order to achieve in music what the Impressionist painter accomplished with color and light. He used five and six tone scales as well as the more traditional diatonic and chromatic scales; he revived interest in the medieval modes of the Gregorian Chants; and he introduced dissonant chords, complex rhythms, and a new musical syntax. But most interesting of all, at least for this particular study, is the fact that Debussy believed one should trust the ear rather than traditional form to determine what is harmoniously good or appropriate. This had the same liberating effect for musical composition as Cézanne's trust of the eye rather than compositional forms had for painting. Even though Impressionism represented no clear break with Romanticism and Western traditionalism, it did produce important innovations which were incorporated in the radical break to follow.

Contemporary music begins at the turn of the century with the advent of two movements: the Expressionism of Schoenberg and the Primitivism of Stravinsky. Expressionism in both music and painting represents a conscious effort to break from the confining structure of traditions. It is the search for a new order which can convey a new experience, a new meaning. In music, Expressionism signifies a revolt against the objectivism of the Impressionists and against the subjectivism of such "late" Romantics as Richard Strauss, Gustav Mahler, and Jean Sibelius. Expressionism, in short, is the attempt to overcome the subject-object dilemma by the development of a new understanding of music itself—its nature and its function.

Early Expressionism in music is dominated by Arnold Schoenberg of Vienna. Schoenberg's approach to composing is not unlike that of Kandinsky's to painting; for both men there is an inner necessity which must receive expression. "In composing I decide only in accordance with feeling, with a feeling for form. This tells me what I must write, everything else is excluded."[17] It is interesting to note that in 1910 in Vienna both Kandinsky and Schoenberg exhibited paintings, and Kandinsky remarked with approval on Schoenberg's attempt in his painting to unite inner and outer vision. It is this same attempt which dominated his music for the rest of his life. Schoenberg realized, according to Kandinsky, that,

the greatest freedom of all, the freedom of an unfettered art, can never be absolute. Every age achieves a certain measure of this freedom but beyond the boundaries of its freedom the mightiest genius can never go. But the measure of freedom of each age must be constantly enlarged. Schoenberg is endeavoring to make complete use of his freedom and has already discovered gold mines of new beauty in his search for spiritual harmony. His music leads us into a realm where musical experience is a matter not of the ear but of the soul alone—and from this point begins the music of the future.[18]

Although Kandinsky's judgment may now seem effusive, his prediction was accurate. In 1911 Schoenberg effected a complete reorientation of tonal patterns. The "system" which emerged from the tonal experimentation is, ironically enough, called "atonal." Schoenberg's atonality really means that there are twelve basic tones of equal importance, and all of these are available to the composer as he desires. Thus, the composer no longer writes an opus in C-major or G-minor, for example, and can see no justification for a necessary central tonality, a central key feeling. Dissonance is no longer utilized to express distress, agony, or some other "disharmony" in experience of the world, nor is consonance used to express peace, tranquility, or some other harmony in the world order. Atonality endeavors to avoid the logical clichés of traditional form by providing its own twelve-tone composition in which relative words like "dissonance" and "consonance" are not simply unnecessary but unintelligible. While Schoenberg did free the composer from traditional and academic forms of music, he did not really free him from imposed structure; for the twelve-tone system, though it has many millions of possible tone series, still prescribes with mathematical precision the progression of any composition melodically and harmonically. Once the pattern of twelve tones is established, it must be religiously followed if the composition is to have a recognizable integrity. One of the finest examples of Schoenberg's freedom and structure in composition is *Pierrot Lunaire* in which Schoenberg combines a speaking voice and a chamber ensemble of five performers.

A contemporary American example of such composition can be found in Vincent Persichetti's *Shimah B'Koli* (Psalm

130). This piece is written atonally and ametrically, without key signature and without bar lines. It would seem that Mr. Persichetti, by freeing himself from any conventional system of composition, hopes to free the listener from his conventional passive or analytical role for an active involvement with the music and the text—the power of the Psalmist's words of despair (Out of the depths have I cried unto Thee) must not be permitted to fail because they are framed by an artful fugue.

Igor Stravinsky's contribution to the revolution against traditionalism came in a variety of different forms over a period of years, the first of which is Primitivism. It is Stravinsky who bequeathed to contemporary music its exciting new concepts of rhythm. From the intricate rhythms of his own ballet music, e.g., *The Firebird, The Rite of Spring,* and *Petrouchka,* we have been made aware of the centrality of rhythm and have had our rhythmic sensibilities sharpened. Through his skillful use of rhythmic devices, Stravinsky reminds us of the primitive, barbaric, sometimes savage nature of our past and awakens in us a recognition of its continuing presence. Spontaneity more than system is expressive of the vitality of life; awareness of the present is more important than anticipation or recollection. "Music is the sole domain in which man realizes the present. By the imperfection of his nature, man is doomed to submit to the passage of time—to its categories of past and future—without ever being able to give substance, and therefore stability, to the category of the present."[19]

Stravinsky also achieves this sense of the present by his use of polytonal harmony in which two or more independent tonalities are used at once to achieve a desired descriptive or emotional effect. This is unlike Schoenberg's twelve-tone system, for polytonal harmony is only incidentally, never systematically, used. Combined with this new harmonic form is the new use of orchestration—new combinations of instruments, new combinations of tonal values, and most notably the use of extreme registers for instruments—all of which produces the excitement and sense of the present so characteristic of Stravinsky's music and so lacking in traditional Western composition. "We find ourselves," writes Stravinsky in 1939, "confronted with a new logic of music that would have appeared unthinkable to the masters of the past. And this new logic has opened our eyes to riches whose existence we never suspected."[20] It is to this man and his revolutionary genius that such composers as Bartok, Block, Hindemith, Milhaud, and Kodaly owe so much in the development of their own gifts.

American Jazz in a more limited way also made its contribution to the liberation of contemporary music both in the United States and abroad. Its improvisations, its graphic emotional descriptions, its polyrhythmic innovations, its blues forms, its progressive forms, all aided the musician in expressing a reciprocity between life as he lived it and music as he played it. The simplicity (often expensive) of its style, the directness and frankness of its motivation, and the involvement of the jazz performing artist established a new form of direct communication with the audience so fundamentally "human" that it had immediate acceptance around the world. In the jazz idiom one can move freely from the direct simplicity of Louis Armstrong to the sophisticated rhythmic experimentation of Dave Brubeck. As a consequence, its influence has been extended to what we once called "the more serious music," and vice versa.

The Expressionist revolt has had profound effect on contemporary music as it has had on contemporary art, and the similarity does not end with the indication of influence. Music, like art, has its representational and nonrepresentational schools, its expressionists and its "abstract expressionists." The word "abstract" in music ordinarily denotes any work which does not have some extra-musical association—a Bach fugue, for example, as opposed to Mussorgsky's *Pictures at an Exhibition*. In applying the borrowed term "Abstract Expressionism" to music, I intend to identify that music which is electronic, automatic, mathematical, or chance composition, music which forgoes the creative genius of the composer for the mathematical machinations of the computers. Because this group, like their painter-counterparts, is the most startling and defiant, we shall begin with them.

The two composers whose works provide the most striking examples of Abstract Expressionism are the contemporary American composers Milton Babbitt and John Cage. Milton Babbitt composes on a giant synthesizer which electronically records and produces any individual tones or combination of sounds which Babbitt desires. In one sense this gives him absolute freedom of choice and at the same time absolute control. The synthesizer is capable of producing all sounds, not just those of the diatonic or chromatic scales, and of incorporating them in his composition. The result is an expression of music, or sound, which is capable of involving the listener on many levels of the conscious and subconscious. Richard Kostelanetz finds analogous forms to Babbitt's compositions in symbolist poetry in which, ideally, each word relates to the other words in a maximum number of ways; or in Joyce's *Finnegans Wake* in which several stories are told at once on the same page; or in the early films of Orson Welles in which each event has many perceptual dimensions.[21] Babbitt's music becomes an event rather than just another interesting composition; it involves an active response from the listener even if that response is rejection.

It may be hard to think of electronic music as an expression of the search for a New Humanism, and yet certain aspects do apply: simply the fact of its innovative form, its freedom to defy musical tradition, is one; its attempt to speak with musical integrity to a technological age is another; and its inherent affirmation of life in the technological age is yet another. Such music can be considered truly antihumanist only by the classical standards of traditional (Greek) humanism. The lasting contribution of such music is impossible to evaluate. Our historical focus on the present is too short.

John Cage has developed a form of composition called "Indeterminacy." It is random writing, music by chance in which even the imperfections on his composition paper may govern the placement of notes. Cage admits that such Indeterminacy opens him to the charge of Dadaism in music. Whether this can be substantiated or not, it is true that Cage studied with Schoenberg and was influenced by the Dada artist Marcel Duchamp, the poet Gertrude Stein, and the philosopher Ludwig Wittgenstein.

Cage's compositions of Indeterminacy affirm the same kind of revelation that the Abstract Expressionist makes possible: the acceptance of what-is, without any qualifications or reasons other than its very being. Consequently his works are full of all sorts of sounds, e.g., the smashing of chairs, gargling, the crunching of raw carrots, but also full of silences of all lengths. "Silence which can never become absolute, is as much a component of music as intentional sound; therefore all the unintentional noises that arise during a performance are parts of the piece."[22] What Cage is endeavoring to show us is the importance of the awareness-of-presence, an awareness of what is happening all around us which we simply take for granted. The most significant musical creation then becomes one's own life in harmony with the world. Cage writes.

The novelty of our work derives therefore from our having moved away from simply private human concerns towards the world of nature and society of which all of us are a part. Our intention is to affirm this life, not to bring order out of chaos nor to suggest improvements in creation, but simply to wake up to the very life we're living, which is so excellent once one gets one's mind and one's desires out of its way and lets it act of its own accord.[23]

Music for John Cage is an existential happening in which form is considered function. Time becomes important, for one has become personally involved. One is now asking, "What is happening?" not "What is the structure, the configuration, of the composition?"

The second major form of contemporary music stemming from the Expressionist revolt has been called by a variety of names which reflect the stages through which it has passed. In general, however, it is "Representational," utilizing recognizable themes, melodies, and harmonics. Between the First and Second World Wars, the term "Neoclassicism" was used by many composers and critics, e.g., Ferruccio Busoni, Stravinsky (again), Aaron Copland, Roger Sessions, to describe a reaction against the extreme forms of Expressionism which began to emerge. Roger Sessions gave this group its credo in 1927:

Young men are dreaming of an entirely different kind of music —a music which derives its power from forms beautiful and significant by virtue of inherent musical weight rather than intensity of utterance; a music whose impersonality and self-sufficiency preclude the exotic; which takes its impulse from the realities of a passionate logic; which, in the authentic freshness of its moods, is the reverse of ironic and, in its very aloofness from the concrete preoccupation of life, strives rather to contribute form, design, a vision of order and harmony.[24]

In short, it was a return to eighteenth-century forms. Although Neoclassicism was followed with a vengeance for a short period of years, its evangelical fervor cooled and balance was restored. Certainly there has been a return to form and structure—as one can see in the works of such a variety of composers as Charles Ives, Aaron Copland, Ralph Vaughan Williams, Benjamin Britten, Dmitri Shostakovitch, Ernest Block, and Ned Rorem—but this utilization of form is not form for form's sake. It does not, as Sessions suggests, exclude the exotic. What the Expressionist movement has really done is to free the composer from the tyranny of form so that he might utilize whatever form he needs to produce, as Sessions rightly suggests, "an entirely different type of music."

This freedom in which everything is admissable is like the new freedom of the painter. He may adopt form when it suits him; he may violate or ignore it for the same reason. Creation is confined only to the nature of the composer's genius. Charles Ives, for example, has scored his *Fourth Symphony* for three conductors rather than one and has included in his composition bits of folk music, hymns, marches, bugle calls—Americana, if you like. Such creativity, vitality, and innovation are grounded in freedom.

This free eclecticism is even found in the rock-and-roll music of such talented groups as the Beatles and Herman's Hermits. Bach and the Big Beat can become the fascinating and striking medium for a song of contemporary social protest. The awareness of time, of the world, of presence, means the emergence of music which, sensitive to and expressive of the human predicament, tries to speak meaningfully within that context.

Peter Yates in *Twentieth Century Music* speaks of the "American Experimental Tradition." Perhaps this is too bland for any permanent designation, but it is at least more accurate than "Neoclassicism" which is contrary to the central development of contemporary music. It would be virtually impossible to compose for the contemporary world without acknowledging one's indebtedness to the Expressionist and Primitivist revolts. Peter Yates states that,

Stravinsky by the decade but Schoenberg by the half-century transformed the past of music in the direction of the present. Stravinsky from decade to decade preserved his lead, his independence, free of tradition, transforming and endorsing the new proposals of music as he understood them, the master, like Picasso, towards whom all fashion turned, himself always ahead of and the maker of that fashion; and in the end he accepted what seemed to be the ultimate product of that half-century (Schoenberg's tone-row), transforming and endorsing it again to his own purpose.[25]

Stravinsky never rejects tradition; he transforms it.

Turning now to the consideration of literature, the problem becomes more complex, the movements more difficult to distinguish and describe. This is true for two reasons. First of all, literature, more than painting and music, has always had man—his life, values, joys, sorrows, accomplishments, defeats—as its central focus. It is, of all the arts, the most inherently humanistic. Therefore, to say that we are engaged in a search for a New Humanism may be misleading at this point. If "humanism," as we have used the word, means to be concerned primarily about man's total context of existence, then what we are searching for is not a New Humanism so much as a new expression, a more meaningful, relevant expression of man-in-context.

The second aspect which distinguishes this art form from the previous ones is that literature is always denotative, never simply connotative. Thus in trying to assess literature —its correlation with music and art and its contributions to a New Humanism—one has not only to contend with a multiplicity of forms, e.g., novel, poetry, drama, essay, short story, one also has to consider and evaluate content. Thus it can happen, as in the instance of the contemporary writer Bernard Malamud, that the human pathos of his novel *The Assistant* can mirror the contemporary religious anguish of the alienated, the disinherited, while at the same time can represent a nineteenth-century style of development, form, and construction.

As a result of these two major considerations, many fine scholars believe that any attempt to classify literature as we have painting and music is either impossible or worthless. The evidence for such arguments is impressive, backed up with suggestions of thematic possibilities or evolutionary lines, e.g., to understand T. S. Eliot one needs (among others) to know Ezra Pound; from here the line leads to Laforgue, Baudelaire, Poe, Whitman, *et al.*

Nevertheless I am convinced that, granting exceptions, one can speak with some assurance about broad movements in literature which do correlate in content, style, or both, with the other art forms; that at the turn of the nineteenth century changes took place in literature which are as dramatic and influential as the Expressionist movements in painting and music. The terms of reference are different, but the changes are similar.

The opinion that genuine changes have taken place is shared by Richard Ellmann and Charles Feidelson, Jr. In their recent anthology *The Modern Tradition* they state in the Preface:

If we can postulate a modern tradition, we must add that it is a paradoxically untraditional tradition. Modernism strongly implies some sort of historical discontinuity, either a liberation from inherited patterns or, at another extreme, deprivation and disinheritance. In any essay on "The Modern Element in Modern Literature," Lionel Trilling singles out a radically anti-cultural bias as the most important attribute of the modern imagination. Committed to everything in human experience that militates against custom, abstract order, and even reason itself, modern literature has elevated individual existence over social man, unconscious feeling over self-conscious perception, passion and will over intellection and systematic morals, dynamic vision over the static image, dense actuality over practical reality. In these and other ways, it has made the most of its break with the past, its inborn challenge to established culture. Concurrently, it has been what Henry James called an "imagination of disaster." Interwoven with the access of knowledge, the experimental verve, and the personal urgency of the modern masters is, as Trilling also finds, a sense of loss, alienation, and despair. These are the two faces, positive and negative, of the modern as the anti-traditional: freedom and deprivation, a living present and a dead past.[26]

By "modern" Ellmann and Feidelson indicate they mean such writers as Yeats, Joyce, Eliot, Lawrence, Proust, Gide, Mann, Rilke, and Kafka. It is an age which terminated about the time that World War II ended and the Cold Wars began. But in order to see this in perspective, we must go back into the nineteenth century to the Romantic movement in literature.

Against the Classism of such writers as Racine, Moliere, Pope, Addison, and Swift, whose work studiously avoided any personal references while generally concentrating on society's nature, structure, and condition, the Romantic movement represented a reaction in terms of an emphasis on the individual. Men such as Wordsworth, Byron, Shelly, and Keats ". . . asked us to be interested in themselves by virtue of the intrinsic value of the individual: they vindicate the rights of the individual against the claims of society as a whole—against government, morals, conventions, academy or church."[27]

The Romantic was a rebel against the fixed, mechanistic concept of order which would deprive man of his power of choice, his moral dignity, and thereby his human excellence.

The Romantic movement, while rebellious, was not a revolution. The Romantic writer did not challenge structure, order, and design; he only challenged their disproportionate importance in our understanding of society, ourselves, and the world. Thus Wordsworth's "Happy Warrior" is a man of reason who "Finds comfort in himself and in his cause;/And, while the mortal mist is gathering, draws/His breath in confidence of heaven's applause. . . ." The Romantic did not so much disavow the emerging experimental sciences as he believed them to be only partial and inconclusive. Reality could be apprehended much more directly and faithfully through an art form.

The Romantic movement, because it was a "pendulum" reaction, resulted in excesses of subjectivism and emotionalism and, consequently, in the counter movements of Naturalism and Victorianism. The difference between these two reactions was not so much a shift in metaphysics as it was a shift in form and style. The transition from Wordsworth and Byron to Carlyle, Tennyson, and Browning or to Hawthorne, Whitman, and Emerson is not all that dramatic.

It is at this point, against this ordered, trustworthy, personally responsive universe that the revolution came. It is here that the "historical discontinuity" which Ellmann and Feidelson note marks the beginning of the Modern tradition. This discontinuity is more than a distinction in style; it does represent a metaphysical shift, a change in point of view which finds not only the world but man himself as strange and unknown. Maurice Friedman, writing of such a shift in *Problematic Rebel* states: "If one wishes to make a decisive break with the universal 'human nature' of earlier philosophy and attain a picture of man in his uniqueness and his wholeness, one must move from *concepts* about man, no matter how profound, to the *image* of man."[28]

Two of the most notable authors initiating this radical

shift are American, Melville and Poe. It was Melville's *Moby Dick* that shocked the sensibilities of self-righteous America. To Starbuck's remark that it seems blasphemous to take out one's vengeance on a whale, Ahab replies:

All visible objects, man, are but as pasteboard masks. But in each event—in the living act, the undoubted deed—there, some unknown but still reasoning thing puts forth the mouldings of its features from behind the unreasoning mask! If a man will strike, strike through the mask! How can the prisoner reach outside except by thrusting through the wall? To me, the white whale is that wall, shoved near to me. Sometimes I think there's naught beyond. But 'tis enough. He tasks me; he heaps me; I see in him outrageous strength, with an inscrutable malice sinewing it. That inscrutable thing is chiefly what I hate; and be the white whale agent, or be the white whale principal, I will wreak that hate upon him. Talk not to me of blasphemy, man; I'd strike the sun if it insulted me.[29]

Fyodor Dostoevsky was another writer who shattered the Romantic concept of man by substituting a descriptive image of man with all his libido showing:

The more conscious I was of goodness and of all that was "good and beautiful," the more deeply I sank into my mire and the more ready I was to sink in it altogether. . . . I got to the point of feeling a sort of secret abnormal, despicable enjoyment in returning home to my corner on some disgusting Petersburg night, acutely conscious that that day I had committed a loathsome action again. . . .[30]

This is the underground man of whom we hear so much more in the writings of the existentialists; it is certainly not the image of the man destined to inhabit Victoria's Crystal Palace, or the image posted on the door of Ellis Island.

Edgar Allen Poe is important, for the translation of his works by the French poet Baudelaire gave rise to the Symbolist movement in French literature. It is this literary ground more than any other which is responsible for our Modern tradition. Edmund Wilson summarizes the Symbolist doctrine as follows:

Every feeling or sensation we have, every moment of consciousness, is different from every other; and it is, in consequence, impossible to render our sensations as we actually experience them through the conventional and universal language of ordinary literature. Each poet has his unique personality; each of his moments has its special tone, its special continuation of elements. And it is the poet's task to find, to invent, the special language which will alone be capable of expressing his personality and feelings. Such language must make use of symbols: what is so special, so fleeting, and so vague cannot be conveyed by direct statement or description, but only by a succession of words, of images, which will serve to suggest it to the reader.[31]

Such a creed has a remarkable resemblance to the creeds of the early Expressionists in painting and music. There are symbolic shades here of the painter Vincent VanGogh and the musician Claude Debussy. It gave rise to a freer style in which rules and forms were subject to alteration, so that an author could achieve whatever effect he desired; the natural and unnatural were often mixed; a variety of solutions to man's dilemmas appeared possible, for the omniscient author began to disappear; vignettes and episodes replaced lifetimes and eras; dialogue and introspection increased; the author, directly or indirectly, became a social, cultural, and spiritual critic in the search for an authentic image of man.

One of the best examples of writing affected by such symbolism is that of Franz Kafka. In one novel Kafka uses a castle, which mysteriously dominates the life of a neighboring village, as the symbol of "God" or "Grace" which man in the village spends his life futilely endeavoring to contact. In another novel, life is described in terms of a phantasmal trial, the only evidence for which is a growing guilt for an unknown crime. The technique of ambiguity in each case is representative of the Symbolist style: either there is God (or "Meaning"), and we cannot reach Him; or there is no God, and life is absurd. In either case, futility is the mark of human existence. Perhaps Kafka's most graphic expression of symbolism comes in his story "The Metamorphosis" in which the image of man himself is the focal point. Gregor Samsa is transformed from the self-image he had prepared for public presentation into the hideous form which he had, in reality, become:

As Gregor Samsa awoke one morning from a troubled dream, he found himself changed in his bed to some monstrous kind of vermin. He lay on his back, which was as hard as armor plate, and, raising his head a little he could see the arch of his great, brown belly, divided by bowed corregations. The bed cover was slipping helplessly off the summit of the curve, and Gregor's legs, pitiably thin compared with their former size, fluttered helplessly before his eyes.[32]

The critical distance between this story and the contemporary dramatist Ionesco's play *Rhinoceros*, in which human beings become rhinos, is not nearly as great as the span of years.

From this Symbolist movement two traditions developed, just as in painting and music. One is called simply the Modern tradition which includes such writers as Yeats, Joyce, Eliot, Stein, Auden, Faulkner, Hemingway, Miller, Sartre, Camus, *et al.*; the other is the "Dadaist" movement which had devotees in Russia, Holland, Spain, Italy, and France, but few, if any, in Britain and America. "The Dadaists," writes Edmund Wilson, "were themselves, as time went on, to turn social-revolutionary: their savage spirit of opposition found a new field in political journalism. And, discarding the name of Dadaists though still intent on the destruction of conventional literature, they took to automatic writing which they called 'Surréalisme.' "[33] One is tempted to include as legatees of the Dadaist movement such contemporary writers as Eugene Ionesco (*The Bald Soprano*), Samuel Beckett (*The Play*), or Arthur Adamov (*Ping Pong*). In the absurdity of their writing, one finds a revolt against the tyranny of banality in the modern theater. We find characters placed in ash cans, in urns, or in bogs; symbols are deliberately confused or contradictory; dialogues have degenerated into a series of monologues and *non sequiturs;* there is no direction, "message," or moral; there is only a pause as the end. But such a judgment would not do justice to the larger contributions of these men, or to the fact that each of their works should be understood more in terms of a protest against "conventional humanity" rather than just conventional literature. These writers are really part of the group we termed the Modern tradition.

The Modern tradition of British-American writing is the amorphous result of two literary traditions and two philosophical traditions: it is Symbolism tempered by Naturalism, existentialism tempered by pragmatism. Pure and adulterated forms of all appear, but common ground is found in the sense of cosmic exile. The Modern tradition describes and dramatizes the loss of orientation and the loss of meaning detailed in the first chapter of this book. It is not so much an expression of evil as it is an expression of the disintegration of faith, values, and tradition. It is an exposure of man's social and political isolation in an indifferent world and of man's alienation and estrangement in a crowded world. The Modern tradition describes a homeless man living in a desert, bearing no distinguishing marks, except perhaps that of Cain.

T. S. Eliot, the poet, sees us as "The Hollow Men" whose heads are stuffed with straw. In death we are not to be remembered as the lost violent men but only as the hollow men, the stuffed men. Albert Camus sees us as superficial, ego-centric silhouettes who simply live "in a way," "on the surface of life, in the realm of words as it were, never in reality. All those books barely read, those friends barely loved, those cities barely visited, those women barely possessed."[34] In death we are not to be remembered as courageous, good men: "A single sentence will suffice for modern man: he fornicated and read the papers."[35] Archibald MacLeish, the dramatist, finds man in a world governed, if at all, by a sightless, irresponsible, unresponsive God; suffering is the only meaningful education man has into the nature of reality and away from the delusion that beauty and love are his destiny.

> What once was cuddled must learn to kiss
> The cold worm's mouth. That's all the mystery.[36]

In death there is no answer to man's predicament and no meaning:

> Shall I tell you how it ends?
> Shall I prophesy? I see our
> Smug world-master on his dung heap,
> Naked, miserable, and alone,
> Pissing the stars. Ridiculous gesture!—
> Nevertheless a gesture—meaning
> All there is on earth to mean:
> Man's last word . . . and worthy of him![37]

With the Modern tradition we seem to have reached the final expression of Baudelaire's suppositions that the only way for modern man to pray is to blaspheme, the only way to live is to hurt, the only way to act is to remain passive.

This existential absurdity and despair is not the end of the pilgrimage, for contemporary literature is more affirmative, more sensitive to human values. The Modern tradition is not the end of an era so much as it is the necessary negation, the declaration of freedom, which precedes a more constructive search for a new statement of human values. Ihab Hassan writes:

The contemporary novel . . . may point to us the way down and out. America is the breeding ground of contradictions. But these are not only its own; they are also those of Western history. The cry which still resounds in the West is Nietzsche's cry when he proclaimed, nearly a century ago, that God was dead. In a sense, all modern literature is the attempt to grapple with this radical insight. And in a sense, too, all modern morality is the attempt to face and to overcome nihilism. "Why has the advent of nihilism become necessary?" Nietzsche asks. "Because the values we have had hitherto thus draw their final consequnece; because nihilism represents the ultimate logical conclusion of our great values and ideals—because we must experience nihilism before we can find out what value those values really had. We require, at some time, new values."[38]

It is my belief that for at least a portion of our contemporary authors—those who are not still wallowing in the bogs of existential despair—there is a real attempt to express something which is meaningful. Of course, some of those writers who belonged to the Modern tradition have moved with the times into a new phase of their own work. This is true of such men as Eliot (*Four Quartets*), Auden (recent poems), Hemingway (*The Old Man and the Sea*), Salinger (*Franny and Zooey, et al.*), Jean-Paul Sartre (*Words*), e.e. cummings (*six nonlectures*). But other names and concerns are new. Of course one could argue that the affirmation expressed by these writers is not new, not a development out of the counsels of despair, but simply a reaction to that despair. An authoritative judgment about the validity of either claim has not been made nor can it be made for years, yet the evidence seems to support the emergence of a more sophisticated, less pretentious, humanism.

Contemporary American poets provide plausible documentation for such a tentative judgment. With the social protest movements of the 20's and 30's over, the poet Paul Carroll believes that one is now left with the "terrible search" for honesty. The artist must now confront himself with the basic question: "Who am I?" "My own poems are attempts, the only way I have, to make sense out of my own existence and the world around me and to understand who I am and what my friends are involved in."[39] John Logan believes that poetry is more religious than it was: "By this I mean the sense of the transformation by art of the natural event into something of beauty and of an enduring transcendent quality, which brings to people a kind of secular grace."[40] LeRoi Jones believes that the whole of experience is open to poetic expression: "I believe that the poet . . . is able, or should be able to take almost any piece of matter, idea, or whatever, and convert it if he can, into something really beautiful."[41] Gilbert Sorrentino believes that it is the poet's task to talk about the world he lives in, not about some abstract idea, and to give it perspective. In all these writers, and others like Ginsberg, Rothenberg, and Rexroth, there is a search for new expressions of language, imagination, and meaning beyond the nihilism of the 20's-40's.

Despite some continuance of the defiant theater of the absurd—"total theater" and "happenings"—Alan Lewis confirms the same shift in contemporary drama. There are

healthy indications today of a return to an affirmation of life and to the search for positive belief. Total negativism may have run its course. Works by Sartre, Brecht, *A Man for All Seasons*, *The Deputy*, are evidences of a return to the dignity of man and a reaching beyond personal despair. In the U.S., the writer feared social commitment. The civil rights movement may now have marked the turn. Young people are no longer a generation without a cause. *Blues for Mr. Charlie* (1964) is a plea for recognition of guilt, which can clear away the obstacles to the fraternity. *After the Fall* is a re-evaluation and a rejection of past claims to a better way of life, but also an honest pursuit of new values and a discovery of hope in the willingness to begin anew. Lorraine Hansberry's (2nd play) *The Sign in Sidney Brustein's Window* is an acid comment on intellectual pretense and a call for renewed faith in the idealist.[42]

The search for meaning, freedom of expression, a New Humanism, is evident in contemporary fiction as well as drama and poetry. Marcus Klein calls it "the age of accommodation"; it is the adjustment of contemporary man to social realities; it is the rejection of the age of alienation. Accommodation is the "mood that occurred when rebellion had exhausted itself, when suddenly the manner in which the individual—the intellectual, the writer, any man—might meet society was no longer so certain, when there was no politics to speak of and when there were no orthodoxies to speak of to restrict one's freedom, and when all theories of society had been shattered."[43] We live in a culture in which there is a self-conscious effort to create new values or to redefine the old ones. Thus in the writing of Baldwin, Kerouac, Mailer, Bellow, Malamud, Updike, Salinger, McCullers, Capote, *et al.* one discerns a renewed desire to communicate, to reach out, to engage the world in an honest dialogue about man's sense of worth, his responsibility, his need for community. Though it recognizes no creed, the quest is a religious one in the sense that its concern is total—involving the whole man. As Ihab Hassan suggests, these authors are searching for a new sense of meaning.

The direction which each of our witnesses—students, artists, musicians, writers—suggests involves a major change in our thinking. The search for meaning, for a New Humanism, does not begin by first asking, "Where are we going?", though direction is important. Nor does it begin by determining by what laws mankind must go at all, though order is necessary to avoid chaos. The search on the campus and in the culture really begins by asking the twin questions of identity and authenticity. "Who am I?" and "How can I be myself?" For all the New Humanists, the point of contact with reality is the point of immediate personal context. What we truly want to do is to tell people who we are, not what information we have. For this purpose we now turn our attention to the two men whose thought is most influential in the philosophical and theological search for the New Humanism, Martin Heidegger and Martin Buber.

three: The prophets: Heidegger and Buber

WITH SUCH WIDESPREAD development and response to the New Humanism in art, music, and literature, one would expect to find such interests becoming evident in other areas of self-expression and concern. It is, of course, a matter of common and well-documented understanding that "climates" of opinion, change, and crises do exist and do exercise a formative influence on all aspects of human activity and thought—particularly those creative, artistic ones within the disciplines of the humanities.

The contemporary all-inclusive shift away from the System, the Form, and the Establishment toward the individual, interaction, and meaning certainly exemplifies such a generalized influence in our lives. Historiography, for example, is no longer dominated by the search for and examination of the Goals or Ideals of history or of any particular society; nor is it an attempt to discern the Immutable Laws which govern the development of all societies. Many historians are now concerning themselves with the less presumptuous task of understanding the actions and responses of peoples and governments within given political and social contexts. Historians are, for example, more interested in Yalta as an instance of Soviet-British-American diplomacy and power negotiations than as a contemporary understatement of Utopia or as the development of a twentieth-century diplomatic decalogue.

Such a shift away from Absolute Form is likewise evident in the other social sciences, in the psychology of interaction, interrelational sociology, and pluralistic economics. However instructive it might be to examine each one of these in detail, it is more pertinent to look at the philosophical and theological developments and expressions of the contemporary scene, for in these disciplines the changes in the understanding of the New Humanism are themselves explicitly acknowledged, explored, and examined. Though many philosophers and theologians have been instrumental in the movements critical of the absolutism of Western metaphysical monism in its variety of forms, two twentieth-century thinkers have written directly and significantly to the point at issue and have suggested ways in which new thought and new expression might develop: the German scholar Martin Heidegger in philosophical thought and the Jewish scholar Martin Buber in religious thought. Because of the major influence these two thinkers have had on contemporary Western thinking, it is with their contributions that this attempt to discuss the New Humanism will begin.

To make such a claim is not to deny or ignore the extensive contemporary interest in Neo-Thomism or Linguistic Analysis, but it does suggest that both of these philosophical interests are developments within that Greek metaphysical dualism which the New Humanism is endeavoring to escape. Neo-Thomism cannot ignore its indebtedness to Thomas and Aristotle in speaking of universal good and universal truth available to reason. Linguistic Analysis, which confines itself to the study of language's role in the structure of the empirical world, cannot escape the relative world of becoming.

One word of caution, before we look at Martin Heidegger's thought, comes to us from the philosopher himself. What he is doing, he wants us to understand, is *thinking*. For Heidegger this does not mean constructing a great and intricate system; it means a self-exposure, a standing open to "life" which he refers to as *Being*, and an appropriate personal response within that context of engagement. Heidegger believes that such an approach is so radically different (and consequently so difficult to communicate) that it runs the risk of being radically wrong or completely misunderstood. Commitment to such thinking may totally and meaningfully reorient our lives, or it may mislead us not up the civilized garden paths, but into a jungle trail (*Holzwege*) within which we become inextricably lost. Such is the risk. But, any life *lived* is risk, and we have seen the emerging sterility of life passed in Plato's formal garden.

The philosophical revolt against what we have earlier called the System, the Form, the Establishment, appeared dramatically and in strength in the nineteenth century with such figures as Schelling, Kierkegaard, Nietzsche, Marx, and Feuerbach. These men were in revolt against the then dominant philosophical system of G.W.F. Hegel. Hegel maintained that all of reality expresses itself as an absolute all-encompassing scheme which he termed the Absolute Idea. This Absolute includes (and in its unity transcends) the whole of "logic" which describes and regulates the internal relationships of that unity. Consequently, Hegel could maintain that historical processes can really be equated with logical processes. My relationship with my neighbor is subject to the same laws as those which govern my thought.

Thus identity or knowledge of any given thing or event is theoretically possible because of the self-consistency of the Absolute. Within Hegel's logic all things are related dialectically, so that logically any one entity can be derived from another. It is of this relationship that the poet Tennyson reminds us with his flower in the crannied wall, which potentially can tell us "what God and man is." Hegel had produced a magnificent all-embracing System which could account for the continuously developing whole of reality. However, his detractors were quick to point out that such a closed scheme, even if it includes movement, eliminates any genuine uniqueness, novelty, or creativity. In fact, the question arose whether life, i.e., existence, could ever be accounted for solely in terms of System. Certainly Kierkegaard and Nietzsche were vociferous in their denials of Hegel's claims. Writes Kierkegaard at his scathing best:

I shall be as willing as the next man to fall down in worship before the System if only I can manage to set eyes on it. Hitherto I have had no success; and though I have young legs, I am almost weary from running back and forth between Herod and Pilate. Once or twice I have been on the verge of bending the knee. But at the last moment, when I already had my handkerchief spread on the ground, to avoid soiling my trousers, and I made a trusting appeal to one of the initiated who stood by: "Tell me now sincerely, is it entirely finished; for if so I will kneel down before it, even at the risk of ruining a pair of trousers. . . ."—I always received the same answer: "No, it is not yet quite finished." And so there was another postponement—of the System and of my homage.[1]

However, most of the criticisms and denials made by these thinkers and their philosohpical progeny, varied as they are from existentialists to empiricists, are conceived in terms of the metaphysical categories indigenous to the System. Even such an existential radical as Jean-Paul Sartre may be criticized for his use of the traditional metaphysical terms "existence" and "essence" when he couples them together in the descriptive existentialist formula: existence precedes essence. Thus one might make the claim, as Martin Heidegger does, that Sartre has not really escaped the Platonic metaphysical trap he claims to have sprung.

These criticisms-in-kind are really reforms in thought rather than revolutions in thought. Martin Heidegger claims that our quest for an understanding of reality must be far more radical than reforms; it must be the expression of a whole new ontology, a completely new understanding of *Being,* of who I *am* rather than how I am *classified.* This means for Heidegger that we must get behind the metaphysical categories of Platonic thought which have dominated Western philosophical tradition for twenty-five hundred years. As a matter of fact, it means getting behind metaphysics altogether. Alfred North Whitehead has made the comment that the development of Western thought is little more than a series of footnotes to Plato; Heidegger would agree, and believes that we must return to the pre-Socratic philosophers, particularly Heraclitus and Parmenides, in whose thought world process and emergence and individuality are given expression. In general it is an attempt to interpret the nature of reality through an understanding of the interpreter himself. It may be that we can then correct some of the errors resulting from the myopia of our Platonic visions of the Good, the Absolute.

Heidegger's criticism of Plato centers on Plato's theory of ideas. In the *Republic,* Plato tells an allegory of a man chained life-long in a cave who is unable to correctly interpret fire-shadows on the cave wall until he is led to the surface, shown the sun and the "real" world. The man then re-enters the cave with the ability to distinguish between the "real" and the "imitation" worlds and understands for the first time what the origin and nature of the shadows are. The allegory means, of course, that knowledge of the changing, impermanent world of particulars—my every day world of pencils, pots, and politicians—can only be understood when I have attained a knowledge of the real world of ideas which are unchanging and permanent. I can only say: "there is a beautiful woman" if I first know, truly, what beauty is. Such Ideas, such abstract universals as beauty, truth, tree, or pencil, Plato calls Forms and grants them, because of their unchanging permanence, metaphysical reality; they are the real world, the yardsticks for our changing world. However, the analysis is not quite complete. There is for Plato a hierarchy of these Forms which culminates in the Form of the Good. Thus knowledge of the particular is given through knowledge of the Idea or Form, and this, in turn, is dependent upon a knowledge of the Good. The Good is understood to be the unifying and creative source of all that is. In the *Timeaus* Plato states that the Good is "not only, to all things known, the cause of their being known, but also of their existence and their reality."

Three implications of this structure are immediately evident and important to this study. First the ultimate metaphysical reality is that of the Good, so that true knowledge depends upon our comprehension of the Good, i.e., the ground of all that is. Second, only the objects of intellect are understood to be fully real. Therefore, third, the subject (I)–object (*world*) dichotomy which has plagued Western thought is given metaphysical justification and status. Under these conditions a priority is established, which suggests that the further I withdraw from the physical world of time, place, and things, the closer I shall be to understanding and perceiving reality. Christianity, for example, has often utilized this priority in teaching about the fatherhood of God. I do not, according to this tradition, analyze my father in order to understand what God is like. Rather, perceiving the absolute fatherhood of God, I am able to understand what my father should be like. It is Heidegger's contention that these particular concepts have played a formative and formidable role in the development of Western philosophical and theological thought. It has produced what we in the United States might call a philosophical ballpark mentality: "You've gotta buy a program to know the players." So, the Absolute Plan is the key to the transient particulars.

The fundamental relationship between this theory of Ideas and Hegel's Absolute Idea is not hard to discern: one can truly understand a given particular only when one sees it in context, in terms of the whole to which it belongs. Thus identity, meaning, and truth are to be found in that which is unitary, perfect, and self-sufficient, in the Absolute Idea. It was, as noted earlier, this formalized, logically comprehensible world against which Kierkegaard and Nietzsche revolted. Soren Kierkegaard noted that the source of Hegel's gross error (failing to comprehend the true existential nature of reality) was to be found in "one lunatic postulate" in which Hegel identified Being and Thought. As William Barrett suggests, this is to confuse the meal with the menu. Marx, in effect, made the same criticism by noting that Hegel's system ignores the reality of a truly dramatic historical dialectic. But for Heidegger, neither Kierkegaard nor Marx goes far enough in his repudiation of that one lunatic postulate.

Perhaps the best way of approaching Heidegger's reaction to that postulate is through an understanding of his use of the word *Being* (*das Sein*). The problem has been that Western thought has consistently, thanks to Platonic traditions, misunderstood this word "Being." Western thought has taken a verb form, the participle of the verb "to be," and used it as a noun in such a way that the force of its verb origin is completely excluded. "Being" as in the phrase "human being," is simply part of a static classification system. It in no way suggests a dynamic presence-here-and-now. The word *Being* (I shall italicize and capitalize the word to indicate Heidegger's use of the word in distinction from traditional Western usage) has, therefore, become identified with the determination of a thing's essence, its *what*ness, not with a thing's presence, its *is*ness. But reality cannot exclude this latter implication of the word. The word *Being* restores to our understanding of self and the world the reality of time, change, and creativity which Plato dismissed when he relegated them to the world of appearances. It is for this reason that Heidegger entitles his first major work *Being and Time*.

Being, for Heidegger is that dynamic context of *is*ness in which all things (using this word in its most inclusive connotation) participate and meet and by which all things are animated by presence, i.e., by being here-and-now and by being self-revelatory. Thus when I meet another, I am not only aware of his physical presence, but also the presence of *himself*—unless he chooses not to be open, i.e., to withhold who-he-is from me, in which case I say that he is "cold" or "withdrawn" rather than "warm" or "open." Under these conditions he is not fully expressing his *Being*, for he is not, as Heidegger puts it, letting the truth be; he is not letting the truth of his *Being* reveal itself. Of course, in a similar situation, I may not choose to be open to such revelation were it there, but then I would be the one guilty of *Non-being*. Consequently meaning is time-full and historical not timeless and ideal, and so is what we call reality.

But as is already evident, our awareness of *Being* really comes through the awarness of our own existence, which Heidegger terms *Dasein* (being-there). Man is *Dasein*; that is, man is self-conscious-existence who finds himself being-in-the-world-here-and-now. Because of his self-consciousness, man is aware of his expression of *Being* which he neither creates nor determines. However, because of his anticipated death, man is aware of his pending *Non-being*, i.e., Nothingness. My existence therefore is constituted by these two tensions which for Heidegger are infrastructured. The result is a time-full existence characterized by my anxiety about death and my consequent free resolve to exist meaningfully in the always present possibility of death. Filling out flight insurance or risking Labor Day traffic continually reinforce such an observation.

Such an existence Heidegger calls transcendence; it is my self-expression in terms of my historical context and in terms of my possibilities of which I am made aware by my relationship to *Being*. *Being* discloses (reveals) itself to me meaningfully only when I open myself to it rather than when I impose my will upon it. Analagously I can only learn to know my friend when I am prepared to accept him on his own terms. Should I make him conform to my image, I shall never "know" him. Such insight is applicable even to myself: I can only "know" who I am when I stop playing a self-imposed role or mimicking others; I can only know who I am when I freely and openly expose myself to *Being* as I at once encounter and participate in it. That such an action is paradoxical is a problem only for the "Greek" mind of conventional Western thought tied to an ideal, for the mind which believes every man should be Albert Schweitzer and every woman Florence Nightingale.

So man learns from the world (from all that *is*) by surrendering himself to the presence and mystery of everything about him, and in such a context, the context sustained by *Being*, he is able to comprehend and is free to pursue the possibilities of his own existence. These possibilities of which Heidegger speaks are ontological not ontic possibilities, e.g., care, anxiety, resolve, guilt, death, rather than the possibilities involved in any empirical classification, e.g., age, success, power, wealth. The word "ontological" in this context refers to those qualities of *Being* which characterize its time-full expressive nature.

These ontological possibilities are constituents which characterize *my* existence in time and are formative for *my* attitudes toward *Being* and Nothingness, life and death. Because existence and not essence is central, man exhibits his own humanism; he is not simply conforming to some predetermined form or ground or set of essential qualities. *Dasein,* incomplete and time-full as it is, is the ground for the New Humanism. If we are sensitive to the anxiety and mystery of the I-was-not and I-will-not-be context within which we continuously live, then Heidegger has made his ontological point.

On the basis of this argument, it is possible to see why one can speak about a New Humanism in Heideggerian terms. Because of the ontological possibilites which constitute man's existence as *Dasein,* Western tradition—which argues from particular to universal and back—is "reversed." For Heidegger, possibility is prior to actuality. Man is constituted by possibilities whose actual expression in time produces the historical reality we call human existence. Thus authentic man expresses his own humanism in terms of care, anxiety, resolve, etc., rather than an embodiment of traditional humanism expressed in terms of immutable laws, e.g., "thou shalt not kill," or teleological goals, e.g., "liberty and justice for all." What Heidegger seems to have done is to provide contours for the continuously unique relationship engendered between man and man, or between man and the physical world, when time and history are considered with radical seriousness. For this New Humanism, classification and judgment of action are as meaningless as they are impossible in terms of standard sets of criteria. Time-full contingencies defy any absolute ethical calculus.

Meaningful human action is conditioned and informed by two things: a) the world-here-and-now in which I find myself and into which I "throw" myself; and b) my relationship to *Being* through which I become aware of my possibilities. Such action does not imply a subject-object world which I can manipulate for my benefit or the benefit of all mankind; such action is rather the response of my openness to the truth of *Being* in which both I and the world are expressive participants. Authenticity of any action thus depends upon the mutual openness of those involved. For example, in the current civil rights controversy in America, the New Humanism would be obliged to say "No" to the militant Negro demand for complete and instant racial integration "Now!"; just as such Humanism would reject the defiant White response of "Never!" to such demands. Neither of these attitudes takes time, history, or the other person seriously, and neither takes seriously the truth of *Being* in terms of personal responsiveness and care. If the racial situation in the United States and elsewhere is "unethical" for the New Humanist, it is so because of human unresponsiveness resulting in irresponsibility and not because segregation *per se* violates some existing code or ultimate ideal. In terms of what older humanism thought of as systems of right and wrong, the New Humanism is "neutral." It is this "neutrality" which gives the New Humanism its alleged radical reputation in contemporary society. The question I must ask myself is not "Am I behaving decently?" but "Am I open and responsive to this person?"

What we can call authentic action must be predicated in terms of this openness to others as well as an openness to the cultural-historical actualities of the world, e.g., the nature of the adequacy of our relative systems of justice, the educational opportunities and preparation of all citizens, the sophisticated world structures of economics, our mobile social systems, the social and psychological inhibitions and exhibitions of the people involved, etc. The achievement toward which such authentic action moves is not some predetermined utopia or programmed Great Society but is the freedom of interaction for all expressions of *Being,* a mutual openness so that the truth of each participant can be revealed and received. In terms of the racial problem, one can at least say that the New Humanism would seek to eliminate the barriers raised by the artificiality of such a superficial classification as color and would concern itself with the crucial problems of inequality, poverty, and education. In the process of such change, the probability of myriad other changes and new directions is great and unpredictable.

This brings us to a consideration of Heidegger's expression of what we have termed the New Humanism. With only slight modifications, the characteristics are remarkably similar to those we have noted in the expression of the arts. What we termed "authenticity" or "integrity" Heidegger would call "truth." Truth is what is, what presents itself, what reveals itself in the context of *Being.* Thus truth is the natural expression of identity uninhibited by a subjective willfulness or by an imposed order or design. To identify a man as Republican or Democrat, Catholic, Protestant, Jew, agnostic, is to tell me nothing about the truth of this man's *Being.* To talk about truth is not to depend upon terms of traditional propositional verification, e.g., because Socrates is a man, he is mortal as all men are; nor is it to depend upon the subjective comprehension of my mind, e.g., my wife is beautiful because she is beautiful for me. Truth is, as indicated, a characteristic of *Being* as it reveals itself to the world and is received in relationship.

This is the key to Heidegger's understanding of authenticity which represents, as it did for the artists, a reciprocity which exists between myself and the world. The fact that truth is a characteristic of *Being* enables Heidegger to avoid the pitfalls of both the traditional correspondence theory of truth and the coherence theory of truth. For example, in Hume's dualism of subject-object, mind-matter, it has been impossible to establish that the idea "in my mind" in any real way corresponds to the perceived object "out there." Consistency only established a particular functioning of my mind and guaranteed nothing about the external object, the thing-in-itself.

The coherence theory of truth, which accepts as "true" that which coheres within the system of reality as perceived, has proved equally unsatisfactory when allied with a spectator theory of knowledge. While such a theory does permit one to function in a complicated and precise world with certainty (though a "certainty" constantly open to revision), it likewise provides one with no way of bridging the subject-object gap of traditional Western thought. It keeps one at odds with the world and estranged from it, and its assumption of coherence can never be justified.

By switching from an ontic to an ontological understanding of *Being*, Heidegger believes that one can overcome the difficulties posed by the above two theories of truth. As *Dasein*, as a being-here-and-now, I am simultaneously and coincidently aware of myself as I am aware of my relationship to *Being*. Thus I know my identity because it is revealed to me in terms of *Being*, in terms of my ontological possibilities. But, it is also this same *Being* which provides the context for the identity of all else; it is also this same *Being* which provides the context within which I engage the rest of reality. I do not simply desire to love as an expression of my *Being*; I must desire to love *another* as an expression of my *Being*.

On the basis of this, Heidegger asserts what could be called the unitary theory of truth. It is now possible to bridge the gap between myself (my apprehension of the world) and the world, for both of these are grounded in the revelation of *Being*. Because *Being* is a common ground, that which is characteristic of my self-knowledge is likewise characteristic of all knowledge, so that in one sense I am not only the recipient of revelation but also the presenter of that revelation. Because of my openness to *Being*, I am on both sides of what once was the subject-object dualism. The extension of *Being* provides identity, but the limitation of *Dasein* permits error.

Yet, why spend so much time on what seems to be epistemology, a theory of knowledge? For Heidegger such a question would only betray a Platonic mind-set. Truth, as an expression of *Being*, is not relegated simply to the realm of of ideas; it involves the fundamental characteristic of all existence, the authentic expression of *Being*-in-relation. Thus to discuss truth is to discuss authenticity, to discuss my existence-here-and-now. My inhumanity is my failure to open myself to the world or to be open to it. My immorality in the New Humanism is the same failure. The implication of truth for the so-called New Morality is inextricably tied in with this understanding of the New Humanism. Any action of mine which inhibits my open reception of the revelation of *Being* from the world (e.g. I distrust all foreigners) or prevents me from authentically presenting myself to the world (e.g. I shall try to be sophisticated) is immoral. As a matter of fact, either one would be an act of self-negation on my part. To live authentically, to live "morally," believes Heidegger, I must "let the truth be."

The implication of this last statement involves us in the second characteristic of Heidegger's New Humanism, that of freedom. As truth is a characteristic of *Being*, so freedom is a structure of *Being* and the ground of truth. Freedom, for Heidegger, involves a lack of coercion of willful imposition in *Being*'s act of revelation and in the reception of that revelation. However, this does not imply that freedom can be associated merely with human inclination, whim, or wish. In fact, Heidegger does not believe that man possesses freedom as a property, but rather that freedom, as the expression of *Being* in *Dasein,* is really presentation, i.e., man cannot truly be himself unless he is fully (therefore freely) *Being* in the here-and-now. It is through such presentation that man has a history. Freedom is the condition of man's relationships to the world, to "what-is-in-totality." Freedom as the "letting-be" of "what-is" perfects the nature of truth as the revelation of "what-is."

The difficulty one has in isolating "freedom" in Heidegger is the same difficulty one has in isolating it in other forms of the New Humanism, i.e., it has no separate existence or uniqueness which characterizes it in the older forms of humanism. Rather, it is the *expression* of *Being* which we know as the transcendence, the *existence,* of our *Dasein* in the world. Its conditioned identity within *Being* is made evident when the revelation of *Being* is inhibited or when the condition of history as the relationship between *Being* (*das Sein*) and being-there (*Dasein*) is being considered.

The importance of freedom for the New Humanism and consequently, the New Morality, is evident in its organic relationship to truth. Anything which prevents or inhibits the expression of what-is, e.g., love between two persons, is immoral because it is the denial of *Being's* free expression. This is not to condone some notion of free love with its contemporary preoccupation with sex. Free love, uninhibited love is the open, sensitive, and responsive relation to another intellectually, emotionally, spiritually, as well as physically. The point at issue is that no one of these characteristics of love should be inhibited in its fitting and responsible expression.

Some scholars and artists would seem to find in Heidegger and the New Humanism parallels to those Oriental thought forms influenced by Indian Hinduism. There are musical, graphic, and philosophical forms in such thought which seem to give expression to *Being*, which do not identify truth or reality with man's perception but as organic to *Being* itself. While there are no doubt similarities between the two approaches, it would appear, from what limited understanding I have of Far Eastern thought, that certain dissimilarities prevent any immediate identification. The first is that in Heidegger's thought, as opposed to Far Eastern thought, the individuality of the person is not transgressed nor transcended in such a way as to negate it. *Das Sein* (*Being*) never disposes or displaces my *Dasein*, (my being-there). Second, Heidegger insists upon the historical time-fullness of existence; *Being* is expressed in and through time. Far Eastern thought finds time illusory and deceptive.

The third aspect of the New Humanism, affirmation, is integral to Heidegger's thought. Like truth and freedom, it, too, is grounded in and expressive of my *Dasein* and should not simply be considered an attitude which I possess, e.g., the power of positive thinking. Affirmation is grounded in the time-fullness of man's *Dasein* which constitutes the reality of history. Just because history is the expression of man's *Dasein*, it occurs *not* as the realized prescription ordered by past events but as the response of man's present *Dasein* to the possibilities which are his in the context of *Being*. Thus affirmation is expressed in man's creative response to the future, to his potentiality. Such affirmation is not any form of naive nineteenth-century optimism, but it is a recognition of man's responsibility in historical reality whether that leads to tragedy or happiness. History has direction in terms of the potentiality of man's *Dasein*, but the implementation of that direction is man's responsible creative act. Time, therefore, should be understood as the possibility of new and continuous life, not necessarily the destroyer of life; it is the conveyer of possibilities, not the monitor of mere succession. This is the affirmation which Heidegger refers to as the "silent power of the possible."

Affirmation as an expression of Heidegger's humanism is likewise expressed in what he terms "care." Care is a charasteristic expression of *Dasein,* as time-fullness is. *Dasein,* as is evident, is self-concerned. The implication of this self-concern is that I am free for my own potential, I am free for either authenticity or inauthenticity. As one who believes in responsible democracy, I can defy a prejudiced society by supporting open housing and school integration; or, for a variety of private fears or desires, I can keep silent. Both possibilities are open to me. Consequently we can say that *Dasein,* in its encounter with *Being,* is in advance of itself at the same time that it is aware of itself in the present world. With these conditions in mind, Heidegger states that care "throws" us into existence, aware at once of our potential, our present, and our past. It is an affirmation of life lived forward toward our potentialities, even the certain potentiality of death. It is this latter which gives care its expressive power, eliminates the indecisive surrender to chance, and confines our possibilities to finite ones, to a life lived in the here-and-now.

Heidegger terms the "call" of care "conscience." It is instructive to note that conscience is also an expression of authenticity, which illustrates how organic all forms of his New Humanism are to *Being.* Conscience as an expression of care is a call to oneself to be one's potential self rather than simply one-of-the-crowd. As such, conscience is the articulation of *Dasein,* for when conscience calls me, it tells me about myself, about my potentiality, and does so unequivocally. If I disregard such a call and fail to realize my potentiality, I recognize that I am "*Being*-guilty." The result is a death-like nothingness, a meaningless existence as one-of-the-crowd. However, *Being*-guilty does function, paradoxically, in making me aware of my "responsibility" in *Dasein*, i.e., that the character of *Dasein* is not some limbo or oblivion out of which I have emerged. *Dasein* is characterized by its potential and therefore by responsibility. When inauthenticity results in my heightened sense of responsibility, "resolve" is that expression of care which projects me, through my *Being-guilty*, into authentic, responsible, self-*Being*. Resolve is thus the precondition for creative and authentic acts of *Being*. No one who has quit smoking for reasons of health needs further explanation of the strengths and weaknesses of this argument(!)

Such expressions of *Being* as a new understanding of humanism are often more provocative than clear, which is perhaps a necessary condition. *Being* emerges with revelatory power and direction, both of which are in fact and in thought necessarily too elusive for any systematizing. Heidegger himself has recognized the difficulties involved and has set aside, at least for the time, the task of writing a totally new ontology. His emphasis upon the existential nature of existence and his denial of the subject-object dualism seem to preclude the possibility of establishing any ordered ontology.

Heidegger does find meaning in existence, as many others have in his penetrating insights about the nature of existence, of being-in-the-world-here-and-now. He finds in the arts, and particularly in the poetry of Hölderlin, a rejection of the conventional humanism, a strenuous effort to express reality in a new form which shatters the ordered, rational subject-object contexts of classical artistic expression. It is for this deliberate reason that he identifies himself with many who have been dismissed by an insensitive, technological culture as irrational or absurd. It is the poet, Heidegger believes, whose use of language enables him, more than any other, to give voice to *Being* in all its temporal and mystical significance. It is the poet who has most successfully defied the pressures to conform to the "aesthetic attitude"—the nine-teenth-century version of the subject-object dichotomy. Evidence for this judgment is the alienation of the modern poet, a process which Heidegger believes began with Blake and the other Romantics. The contemporary poet does not speak within his age, he rather speaks to it from sources of *Being* itself —an expression of existence from deep within man himself. Thus language, insofar as it articulates my experience of *Dasein,* of being-there, is considered to be the "house of *Being.*" The potentiality of *Being* is realized, in part, by the creative responsible act of articulation. Thus language ceases to be what it has commonly been considered in Western thought: a descriptive device; and it becomes an event. It is for this reason that Heidegger can consider contemporary poetry as historical reality. The poet, more than any other, can bring us with wonder and awe into the presence of *Being;* he can make us aware, as were the pre-Socratics, of the astonishing here-and-now of our eventful lives.

The theological parallel to this philosophical development is remarkable if not in fact identical. The contemporary theological revolt, like its philosophical counterpart, is against Greek metaphysical dualism which has dominated Western theology since the great Church Councils of Nicea and Chalcedon. Greek philosophical thought becomes dominant, then, through Thomas Aquinas and the Reformation to the great orthodox and related systems of Roman Catholicism, Lutheranism, Calvinism, and Anglicanism of the early twentieth century. The mainstream of Western orthodox Christian thought has been charted by creedal statements systematizing the relationship between finite, mortal man and an omniscient, omnipotent, omnipresent God, Creator of heaven and earth, the Redeemer of men.

In terms of such a metaphysical theism, reality and truth—as in Greek philosophy—became identified with an

Absolute System which accounted for its own internal logic. Theologically the System was identified with God and the heavenly kingdom. The Rule or Absolute law was equated with the will of God and the providence of God which governed all creation. To perceive God's will, then, was to perceive his law which governed the mundane affairs of men. Such law was validated by God through revelation and reason given to the Church. The consequent hierarchial systems, fortified by the Sacrament of Holy Orders or Divine Ordination, further isolated the world from God, the unreal from the real, time from eternity, the profane from the holy. For theology the result was a duplication of all the problems philosophy had faced because of the Greek dualism of appearance-reality, thought-thing, subject-object, time-eternity. For Christianity, of course, such a problem became crucial in the Church's attempt to describe Jesus as the Christ, the God-man. The Greek influence, dominant at the great Christological Councils mentioned above, made such a Christological description rationally incomprehensible. The Church simply put together such terms as human and divine, finite and infinite, sinful and holy, mortal and immortal, etc., with the admonition that comprehension of the Person of the Messiah was beyond human understanding. From this period until the present, the Church has struggled to express meaningfully man's experience of a transcendent God within the confines of Greek thought.

Perhaps at this point some statement should be made explaining why a religion emerging from Judaism should become so characteristically Greek. First, its great growth, following its inception in Jerusalem, was in the gentile communities of the Mediterranean world. Second, Christianity began at a time when Judaism itself was being profoundly influenced by Philo, the Jewish Hellenistic philosopher. Third, and most important for us, Christianity had to make its way in a culture intellectually dominated by Greek thought. Thus the great Church Councils mentioned earlier were really defensive in nature, not confessional; the Church was not so much stating what it believed about the Christ as it was trying to defend itself against the intellectual attacks and misrepresentations of Greek intellectualism. The creeds originally were not meant as confessions of faith but as a translation of limitations to guide Greek philosophical inquiries into the nature of Christian belief. Understandably, such preoccupation with metaphysical forms soon became the focus of Western theological thought, and Jewish mysticism and monotheism were lost in logic and metaphysics.

The contemporary theological revolution had its first serious expression in the sixteenth-century revolts of Zwingli, Luther, and Calvin against the ecclesiastical oppression of the medieval Roman Church and the theological oppression of the great Thomistic synthesis. Luther particularly wished to avoid the theologically stifling effects of scholasticism which attempts to account for the whole of a man's life within a rational System of thought.

But again, as at the Great Councils, the force of Hellenistic cultural forms proved too powerful, and the insights of the theologians too incomplete, to effect a genuine revolution in thought. The Reformation was just *that*—and the revolutionary insights were incorporated into the renewed ecclesiastical System of Lutheranism, Calvinism, Anglicanism, and all their Protestant progeny.

The second theological attempt to get back to the dynamic insights of the early Church, to get back behind the Hellenistic pronouncements of Nicea, came in the nineteenth century with Soren Kierkegaard's repudiation of the State Church of Denmark and the stultifying effects of Hegelianism on theological thinking. Kierkegaard did not, as did the Reformers, produce a rival theological System; rather, he set out to confront the life of Christendom with its own expression of faith. The discrepancy between the responsibility of a redeeming community and the lip service offered the world through allegiance to a liturgy was the constant target of Kierkegaard's ironic wit.

For Kierkegaard the reality of faith, and thus the reality of life, can only be known and understood when the individual, as a unique person, stands in awe and dread before God. Religion is not a matter of avowed creedal absolutes but of an ultimate concern which involves my total life—public and private, mental and physical. To live existentially in faith is to be aware that I am, in the totality of my life, continuously being addressed by God. In Kierkegaard the search for a new ontology, a new understanding of being, begins. It is upon this base that Martin Buber and Martin Heidegger build, though Heidegger chooses to ignore the theistic implications of Kierkegaard's thought.

This by no means implies that Kierkegaard's existentialism represents the theological mainstream for Western Protestantism or Catholicism. For Protestantism the main development was a form of post-Hegelian "liberalism." Because of the Hegelian Absolute Idea and its self-expressive, self-consistent logic, which Protestant theologians could identify with God, the problem of what to do with a transcendental God "out there" seemed to be solved by immanence— the indwelling of God in man and the world. God could be found in, and revealed Himself through, man and the evident continuity of all creation. The result of such liberalism was a growing theological anthropology. Religious thought became increasingly identified with secular thought, and the concept of a transcendent God became increasingly irrelevant. Nietzsche was perhaps the first to realize the true implications of such a development, for it was Nietzsche who pointed out to the world that an irrelevant God is a dead God. Theological anthropology became the ground for an emergent philosophical anthropology. The theological insight of Nietzsche have led to the contemporary existential, atheistic humanism of Jean-Paul Sartre and the "radical theology" of the death-of-God theologians.

Within the Protestant mainstream, a "neo-orthodox" reaction opposing liberalism's identification of the emerging kingdom of God with the emerging maturity of man appeared first in the 1920's in the theology of Karl Barth. Barth, understanding the force of Nietzsche's argument and seeing only man's immaturity about him, reasserted as a necessary ground for all Christian thought, the transcendence of God: God is "wholly other"; between God and man exists an infinite, qualitative distinction which only the initiative of God can overcome. That God's "humanity" is evidence in the Christ is a matter of God's revelation, not human reason. The brilliance of his thought and the extent of his influence cannot be denied, yet some would see his *magnum opus, Die Kirkliche Dogmatik,* as the culminating expression of the "old theology," not the herald of the new. His basic theological position reaffirms the Greek metaphysical orientation. Barth has rejected the existentialism which influenced his early thought.

The dialectic with mainstream Protestantism continues with a reaction to "neo-orthodox" thought in the new directions suggested by the late German theologian Dietrich Bonhoeffer and the American theologian Harvey Cox. It is perhaps indicative of the character of these later theologians that they have been loosely termed "neo-liberal." To be more descriptive or more definitive would be presumptuous, and any assessment of final directions or systems would be premature. It is enough, for the purposes of this essay, to note the tradition in which they stand and the basic orientation out of which they speak.

Roman Catholic thought over the same period has remained well within the Greek metaphysical categories. It is true that Thomism has given way to various forms of Neo-Thomism, that there seems to be a revival of interest, particularly since Vatican II, in the thought of Augustine, and that Teilhard de Chardin has interested the theological world in the description of his "Omega point." But, the figures of Plato and Aristotle are still much in evidence in the internal dialectics of the Roman Church.

The search for the New Humanism, the expression of the New Morality does not come out of this so-called mainstream, either Protestant or Roman Catholic. Rather, it emerges from that strain of "underground" theology which begins with Kierkegaard and moves through Nietzsche and Heidegger to any number of contemporary theologians, *viz.*, Bultmann, Ogden, Michalson, Ebeling, and Rahner. Interestingly enough, its most influential and creative twentieth-century exponent is the Jewish scholar Martin Buber. It is Buber's descriptive ontological analysis of the *I-Thou* relationship which had revolutionized theological anthropology and has prepared the way for the New Humanism and the New Morality. As diverse thinkers as Paul Tillich, Rudolph Bultmann, Karl Heim, H. Richard Niebuhr, Donald Baillie, Paul Lehmann, Karl Barth, Carl Michalson, Charles Hartshorne, Henry N. Wieman—the list is endless really—acknowledge a profound indebtedness to Buber's thought.

It is noteworthy, I think, that this brilliant thinker should emerge out of the Jewish religion and that his influence is more profoundly felt in Christendom than it is in Judaism. I believe the first observation to be true, because Christendom recognizes in Buber the authentic prophetic voice in response to which both early Judaism and Christianity have developed. It takes Christians behind the Greek influence of the early Councils to their Hebraic origins. This point introduces the second observation above. Buber's thought has had greater impact on Christian thought than on Jewish thought because the Greek heritage for Christians has necessitated the construction of endless theological "systems" to explain the dual nature of appearance and reality, God and man, good and evil, heaven and earth. Buber's *I-Thou* offers a significant alternative to such systematizing. Because the prophetic tradition for the Jews has always been an ontological one, not a metaphysical one, there has been no theological development in Judaism comparable to that in Christendom. The Torah still stands as the norm of man's relationship to Yahweh, to God, and there is no need for further speculative thought; as a matter of fact, such speculation for the Jews borders on the sacrilegious because of its presumptuousness. However, it is not unimportant to notice here that Martin Buber speaks out of the Hasidic tradition in Judaism, which opposed the Hellenization of Judaism in the third century, A.D., and which militantly opposes the domination of Rabinic legalism —the form of idolatry to which Judaism is most prone.

Martin Buber believes that "all real living is meeting," that "in the beginning is relation," and that this reality is to be understood within the ontological context of being (existence).

Man's threefold living relation is, first, his relation to the world and to things, second, his relation to men—both to individuals and to the many—third, his relation to the mystery of being— which is dimly apparent through all this but infinitely transcends it—which the philosopher calls the Absolute and the believer calls God, and which cannot in fact be eliminated from the situation even by a man who rejects both designations.[2]

Buber begins, as does Heidegger, by attacking the traditional Western theory of knowledge which assumes that the primary problem is overcoming the polarity which exists between myself and the world, i.e., I can't really know the world; I can only know my impressions of it or my own construction of it. To such problems and related ones of the subject-object dualism, Buber responds by suggesting that they are pseudoproblems. Such problems arise because one assumes that the identity of the *I* is self-evident—that we all know who *we* are simply in the act of being. René Descartes' affirmation which emerges from his process of doubting: "I think therefore I am," is a classic expression of this identity *faux pas*. With a dynamic world view, isolation can never be the condition for identity.

It is Buber's belief that *I* is a differentiating word of identity which makes no sense, indeed cannot be spoken, without the correlative words *Thou* or *It* through which and with which I establish my identity. *I-Thou* and *I-It* are primary words from which the *I* of the self is only later abstracted, so that one can say: "I did this" or "I met her" or "I am very happy."

Though man's "living relation" is threefold, which includes a relationship to God, man's relationship to the world is twofold and is characterized by the two primary words just indicated. That is, Buber has recognized that there is a radical qualitative difference between my relationship to others and my relationship to things. Yet even that statement is not exact enough. There is a radical difference between my relationship as an *I* with another *I* and my relationship as an *I* with an *It*, an object or even another human being whom I may treat as an object.

The relationship of my *I* with another person's *I* Buber calls a subject to subject relationship, or (from within the relationship itself) and *I-Thou* encounter. It is this experience which informs me *who* I am rather than *what (I-It)* I am. The *I-Thou* relation, therefore, is the most fundamental human relationship of all. One actually begins within it as a child. A child says *Thou* to its mother before it learns to say

I. Only gradually does the *I* emerge and develop and grow through encounters with others as persons. The psycho-spiritual poverty of persons deprived of love early in life attests to the developmental and creative power of this relationship which involves the total person. Meaning and identity are created in the encounter, so that in a very real sense I am a "different person" in terms of each genuine *I-Thou* relationship that I have. Each relationship has its own creative impact. Thus it is not strange that I find myself a somewhat different person in the relationships which I have with my mother, my wife, my son, and my friend. Each is a creative situation which has its unique meaning, impact, and result. Consistency of "character" or what we loosely call "personality" develops because of similarities induced by our broad culture contacts, e.g., my constant contact with those who come from the Midwest or New York City. Communication media are rapidly extending such "context" to whole countries. Ultimate spiritual identity, however, is the result of my encounter with the eternal *Thou*, God, who meets me in and through all of the *I-Thou* encounters I have with other persons. God is the ground, the possibility of such encounters, just as for Heidegger, *Being* itself is the ground of all temporal existence and meeting.

However, there is an essential difference here between Buber and Heidegger. For Heidegger, one's identity is bound up with one's possibilities and potentialities in *Being*. "Existence" is the realization of one's potentiality in *Dasein*. But it is just here that Buber takes issue with Heidegger. Heidegger's understanding of "existence" is monological not diological: "The man of 'real' existence in Heidegger's sense, the man of 'self-being,' who in Heidegger's view is the goal of life, is not the man who really lives with man, but the man who can no longer really live with man, the man who knows a real life only in communication with himself."[3]

At this point the issue is quite sharply drawn between Buber's understanding of the Eternal *Thou* and the creative process of encounter with others, and Heidegger's understanding of *Being* and the creative expression of my *Dasein* in relation to its potential in *Being*. Heidegger's isolation within *Being* itself Buber sees as an inheritance from Nietzsche. If God be dead, then it follows that man has no one to communicate with ultimately but himself. Buber notes that,

This mature resolute existence with the world knows nothing of an *essential* relation. Heidegger would perhaps reply that it is only the self which has become free that is really capable of love and friendship. But since self-being is here an ultimate, the ultimate, which the existence is able to reach, there is absolutely no starting-point for understanding love and friendship still as essential relations. . . . Existence is completed in self-being. . . . Heidegger's self is *a closed system.*[4]

Buber also believes that Heidegger's ontology does not really represent *Dasein*—"being-there" in all its concrete reality, but rather is an abstraction from that temporal reality. "Life," writes Buber, "is not lived by my playing the enigmatic game on a board by myself, but by my being placed in the presence of a being with whom I have agreed on no rules for the game and with whom no rules can be agreed on."[5]

Because the *I-Thou* relation has to do with my identity and meaning as a person and, as such, involves my total self, the relationship is located in time and place. However, the meaning of the relation transcends such limitation in much the same way that quality transcends the limitation of quantity and is yet dependent on it. Within the relationship I am unaware of anything but the meaning of the encounter; I am not even *self*-conscious in any isolated way. It is only when the *I-Thou* relationship has terminated (as they all must do, intermittently at least, because of our finitude) that

I am aware that *I* participated in such-and-such a relation at this place for that length of time. When I am able to make such an assessment, the relationship has been objectified, has become part of my *It*-world. The *I-Thou* experience for Buber, thus, is similar to Heidegger's sense of "presence" in which I become "open" to the revelation of the truth of *Being*—in this case the *Dasein* of another. Nevertheless, there are some differences even here. For Buber the *I-Thou* encounter is lived in the present, but it is a present experienced in terms of continuous duration rather than continuous "flow." To live in the *It*-world is to live in the past for here nothing really changes but simply stands in relation. For Heidegger one's understanding of time is somewhat different. All authentic *Being* is time-full: man as *Dasein* is open not only to others but also to the physical world. To withdraw from this openness is to live in the past which is, in Heidegger's terms, nonexistence.

For Buber the *I* which is created by this *I-Thou* encounter with others and with the eternal *Thou* is the *I* that then experiences the objective world of *It*. In this objective world, I place my *I* in relationship to some*thing* and thereby experience it and know it. Such objects, which even include such processes as cause-effect, can tell me about myself in terms of *what* I am, but they can in no way advance my understanding of *who* I am. The *It*-world is the technological world, the world of things—Structure, Systems, Organizations, and Relations without which, as a total person, I cannot live. The *It*-world is exceedingly important to my *It*-self—its health, physical and social welfare, etc. The great problem arises when the *It*-world assumes too large a proportion of our time, interest, and energy; or, more devastatingly, when we endeavor to let it perform the function of the *Thou* for our lives. So Buber cautions his readers: "And in all the seriousness of truth, hear this: without *It* man cannot live. But he who lives with *It* alone is not a man."[6]

Any genuine survey of Buber's thought must include some understanding of what he means by the eternal *Thou* and by destiny. The eternal *Thou* is for Buber what *Being* is for Heidegger. Just as every *Dasein* is an expression of *Being* so the eternal *Thou* is "glimpsed" through every particular *Thou*. Fulfillment or consummation of the innate capacity we have for such a relationship can be achieved only with the eternal *Thou* who cannot become an *It*. In this relationship unconditional exclusiveness of identity and the unconditional inclusiveness of relation to reality are one.

In such ontological terms, Buber finds an answer to the transcendence-immanence problem of traditional Western theology. "If you explore the life of things and of conditioned being you come to the unfathomable, if you deny the life of things and of conditioned being you stand before nothingness, if you hallow this life you meet the living God."[7] Such a God can "only be addressed, not expressed." It is in and through this encounter that the destiny of my *I* is fulfilled, not through the cause-effect relations of the *It* word.

What Buber has done is to provide Western theological thought with an escape from the inherent contradictions of its Greek metaphysics. In traditional theology, God is thought of in terms of oneness, perfection, immutability, eternality, omniscience, etc. But this meant that God must know all things now and forever—which meant, in spite of ingenious efforts to overcome it, that man had no genuine freedom, no moral responsibility. The logic of such sovereignty for God forced Calvin to admit that some men were predestined to damnation. Such a traditional view of God in His Hellenistic majesty also implied that God was "impassible," i.e., beyond being moved by sorrow, tragedy, or love. He was Aristotle's

Unmoved Mover or Thomas' First Efficient Cause. Such a concept, in point of fact, destroyed any meaningful relationship, including the relationship of prayer, between God and His creation. The arguments are all too familiar: "Why pray to a God who already knows?" or, "Why pray when the whole thing is already predestined?"

What Buber has done is to recall to Western theology the wisdom of the ontological, Old Testament ascription of God: *I Am*. For Buber the New Testament need not change that insight at all: "How powerful, even to being overpowering, and how legitimate, even to being self-evident, is the saying of *I* by Jesus! For it is the *I* of unconditional relation in which the man calls his *Thou* Father in such a way that he himself is simply Son, and nothing else but Son."[8] In fact, what Buber does is to recall the spontaneity and humanism of the Early Church of New Testament times and of the life of Jesus Himself. It was He, after all, who identified Himself with the prophets rather than the priests; it was He who was not afraid to heal on the Sabbath, to eat and drink with any man he so chose, to associate with the hated Samaritans. Such freedom to love, to relate, to be open to the world is a humanism grounded in an existential ontology and not a Greek metaphysic.

The humanism implicit in Buber's thought is strikingly similar to the New Humanism of Heidegger's philosophy and of the artistic world. Life is real, i.e., authentic, when it is openly engaged with others. "All reality is an activity," states Buber, "in which I share without being able to appropriate for myself."[9] Authentic living is an authentic sharing. The minute I withdraw myself from such encounter with others and make a claim in terms of my individuality, I am isolated, living in the past, and inauthentic. Individuality lives in a fiction of its own special being, its *My*: my kind, my race, my creation, my genius. "The more a man, humanity, is mastered by individuality, the deeper does the *I* sink into unreality."[10]

Freedom is found in the creative fulfillment of my destiny, that is, my openness to the encounter with the eternal *Thou*. Freedom does not participate in the world of *It* which is governed by the laws of causality. But man is not confined to the causal world and, as a matter of fact, leaves it (i.e., transcends it) each time he enters into the world of relation. The mark of man's freedom is his ability to decide, to respond, to *be* in terms of another.

Affirmation is everywhere evident within the destiny of the *I-Thou* relation. It is the *Yes* with which my life is accepted within that relationship; it is the love which is the most characteristic form of it. This affirmation is not an achievement, nor is it a possession, nor is it an acquired trait; it is the expression of my true being to another and his to me. Buber says :

Love is *between I and Thou*. . . . Love ranges in its effect through the whole world. In the eyes of him who takes his stand in love, and gazes out of it, men are cut free from their entanglement in bustling activity. Good people and evil, wise and foolish, beautiful and ugly, become successively real to him; that is, set free they step forth in their singleness and confront him as *Thou*. In a wonderful way, from time to time, exclusiveness arises—and so he can be effective, helping, healing, educating, raising up, saving. Love is responsibility of an *I* for a *Thou*.[11]

four: The new humanism

THE OVERWHELMING impression one gathers from the protests and creative expressions of the students, musicians, artists, writers, philosophers, and theologians is the affirmation of a New Humanism. Lewis Mumford, in *The Arts in Renewal*, sees the artist as one who has the mission to deliver us from madness:

In this [present] situation the artist has a special task and duty: the task of reminding men of the depth of their humanity and the promise of their creativity. Those who have surrendered to the machine, those who have defrauded themselves of their own human inheritance, those who have revolted against the goods as well as the evils of the past, against the benefits as well as the injustices, cannot perform this mission. But those who dare to be truly human, who dare to love and to create out of the fullness of their being may yet deliver the human race from the cold and calculating insanity that now threatens mankind with perhaps universal extermination.[1]

Often, however, as noted in Chapter II, the affirmation is a defiant one without regard for propriety or tradition, and this is one reason for calling the humanism "new." The humanism expressed by these artists and writers does not consciously try to represent some correlation with the past or past expressions of humanism. It functions as vision, and unexpressed first principle, justification for which is unnecessary and impossible. There is no attempt on the part of these various artists and writers to cite the logical necessity or the pragmatic advantages of such a humanism. It is simply *there* and reveals itself in everything which they do. Humanism is not to be accounted for but to be expressed. The poet Charles Olson writes in "Letter 6": "there are no hierarchies, no infinite, no such/many as mass, there are only/eyes in all heads,/to be looked out of."

The philosophers and theologians certainly do not, or cannot, ignore the past, but they, too, want to say something "new" about humanity. As analytical disciplines, they must endeavor to establish the "new" by indicating its position and its stand in relation to prior positions and thought. For that matter, they must face the added difficult task of trying to project new thoughts in old words. Unfortunately, as T. S. Eliot observes in *Burnt Norton,* "Words strain,/Crack and sometimes break, under the burden,/Under the tension, slip, slide, perish,/Decay with imprecision, will not stay in place,/Will not stay still." One assumes that it is for this reason that Heidegger (particularly) has resorted to coining new words to assist in the crucial task of meaningful expression.

But this is not to state just what it is that is being so universally assumed and affirmed. Initially one can say this: the New Humanism affirms the experience of my-being-in-the-world-here-and-now, and that such an experience is complete in itself. The contemporary poet Robert Creely in a headnote to *Words* states: "I see no progress in time or any other such situation. So it is that what I feel, in the world, is the one thing I know myself to be, for that instant. I will never know myself otherwise." It is evident that such a posture reveals a strong existentialist influence; yet at the same time, such an affirmation would seem to deny the priority implicit in the widely accepted existentialist formula of Jean-Paul Sartre, "Existence precedes essence." The New Humanism believes that existence (my "is-ness") and essence (my "what-ness") are coincident, that what is at stake in any given life is not humanism itself but only the *authenticity* with which one's Being is lived. It is possible, according to the New Humanists, for a life to deny such free or open expression, but such a denial is really an act of self-negation. One is living a contradiction: one's inhumanity, one's lack of authenticity, can only be grounded in the power of one's humanity, i.e., one's existence here-and-now.

But such an argument has merely pushed the inquiry back one step further. If the New Humanism is grounded in one's existence-here-and-now, what does such existence mean? By what criteria is it to be understood, particularly as authentic or inauthentic? Acknowledging the insights of both Heidegger and Buber, the New Humanist accepts as a "given" the organic relationship which correlates man and the world and man and man. To exist authentically, then, is to live responsively in the responsive world in which one finds himself. Marcus Klein, in *After Alienation*, notes that the protagonists of contemporary American novels move from the condition of alienation from society toward an acceptance of social responsibility (but not conformity)—"a discovery by these heroes that their destiny lies not in isolation, but rather in joining the social battle in a somewhat existential mode of engagement."[2] It is the world of encounter in which meaning is created in the encounter itself, whether this be with men or things.

It is this creative encounter which gives the term "authenticity" its power and its character, for authenticity (as *word* or condition) implies either a standard of meaning by which a man, an action, or a thing might be judged true or genuine; or it implies a creative engagement from which meaning emerges. For the New Humanist it is the latter. This means that there is no objective criterion in terms of which man might truly measure himself: no ideal, no principle, no Platonic Form, no God-image which could provide an absolute, recognizable, and universal paradigm. Were such a model or measure to exist, it would simply prefigure and thus standardize man, deprive him of his uniqueness, his creativity, his spontaneity, and therefore his meaning. When we do look for guidance to Moses or the Christ, to Gandhi or Lincoln, it is not the "person" but his way of expressing his own authenticity which attracts us. When this distinction is not made clear, we are open to such hilarious arguments as: "one should not smoke because Jesus never did," or "Lincoln wore a beard; so should I." I believe that the poet Charles Olson is making this distinction between "person" and authenticity in "Letter 27":

> There is no strict personal order
> for my inheritance
>   No Greek will be able
> to discriminate my body
>   An American
> is a complex of occasion. . . .[3]

Authenticity as creative engagement also means that man cannot satisfactorily or precisely measure his meaning or meaningfulness in terms of any external laws or divinely dictated imperatives. The objection is the same as that for the absolute paradigm. There simply is none. Were they to exist, such laws or decrees would artifically curtail and control man to the point of "deforming" rather than "informing" his creativity. Robert Kelly wrote of this possibility in his poem "The Alchemist": If we do not act to inform our temporal and spiritual leaders,

> we will walk forever down the hallways into mirrors and
> stagger and look to our left hand for support & the sun
> will have set inside us & the world will be filled with Law,
> and it is that exchange we must sweep out of the temple,
> the changing of gold and power & the figure of Christ into
> Law,
> till the leaf is subject only to the pattern of its own green
> veins[4]

Man's potential for action, expression, and growth would be limited to prefigured possibilities rather than open to the inventive and imaginative responsibility of his own *Being*.

Even the "divine" imperative to love does not alter the point, for love is not a law but a relationship. In fact, much of the confusion in the contemporary undisciplined discussion of "love" as an ethical principle, a rule, an end, a technique, or as motherly, fatherly, erotic, agape, etc., is because the authors involved have failed to distinguished between the denotations and the connotations of their term. Or, the confusion results because they have tried to extend a word which for them adequately describes one form of encounter to many forms of relationship, e.g., if "sweet gentleness" is the accepted definition of love, can one then call parental discipline "love?" Surely not unless the term is broadened or the discipline dismissed. Linguistic Analysis scholars would state that such imprecision simply indicates that the user has not determined what *kind* of word "love" is. Thus the confusion would seem to be in terminology as well as in analysis. The New Humanist uses the term "love" as a synonym for an *I-Thou* encounter, for that openness to the world and to others which permits the authentic relationship to take place. Such authenticity may be expressed in compassion, pity, eroticism, care, responsibility, ad infinitum; love is simply that human response which allows a creative and therefore meaningful relationship to occur. As such it does not prescribe the nature of that relationship, but simply indicates the possible conditions for authenticity.

The New Humanist would equally deny as authentic the poignant declaration of purpose in Alan Paton's *Cry the Beloved Country*:

I shall no longer ask myself if this or that is expedient, but only if it is right. I shall do this, not because I am noble or unselfish, but because life slips away, and because I need for the rest of my journey a star that will not lie . . . I do it because I am no longer able to aspire to the highest with one part of myself and deny it with another.[5]

As appealing as such security and self-righteousness may be, the New Humanist is convinced first of all that such a fixed star belongs to a fictional firmament. There simply is no such external obtainable standard to which man can appeal. Secondly, the thought that such a standard might be available is untenable for the New Humanist, for any absolute standard would preclude his free, spontaneous, creative expression—his responsibility as a human being.

The key word for such authenticity-in-encounter is not The Right, or The Good (or The Truth), but integrity. Man, in his act of totalizing, i.e., comprehending and constructing his world, must not impose, at least without acknowledgment, his wilful or unexamined interpretation upon that world. I must not assume, for example, that democracy as we know and practice it in the United States is necessarily *the* appropriate form of government for every other nation no matter what its history or what stage its socioeconomic development represents. To impose such a system on an underdeveloped nation might be more tyrannical and less authentic than the "enlightened" rule of an oligarchy or junta. Africa and Southeast Asia have provided cases in point. Such an imposition would act to distort reality by avoiding the integrity of the meaningful encounter. My totalizing the world must be my response to the world as it addresses me in all its forms and power.

On the other hand, the converse response must be equally rejected, i.e., I must not simply be the function of the forms and forces which stand over and against me, so that the objective world completely dominates my total human response. It is this situation which results in what some sociologists call the "other-directed" person. One does, thinks, and reflects what one believes and perceives the world expects and demands. Under these conditions I am not my own keeper and could never be my brother's.

The integrity, or genuine encounter, which results in authenticity involves a tension between the poles of extreme subjectivity, in which I seek to act in isolation, and extreme objectivity, in which I am only acted upon. Otherwise, it is neither meeting nor engagement but either imposition or conformity. As long as tension exists between my imposition upon the world and the world's imposition upon me, so that real encounter may occur, authenticity is possible, creativity is possible. In fact, the New Humanist maintains that where such a genuine encounter *does* occur, authenticity *does* result, and creativity *is* realized.

The "measure" of authenticity, as an indication of the totality of engagement, is thus the expression of what can now be called "truth." I am acting with integrity when I am responding to the world with the totality of my being. It is under these conditions that I can be called "responsible," i.e., able to respond openly, freely, and creatively with all that engages me. Such responsibility can even entail the will-ful acceptance of a set of laws or rules for my guidance or can equally entail my rejection of some existing standard which denies my responsibility.

This raises the question of the distinction between the authentic situation and the authenticity of the self. Part of the risk of *Being*, of living life under the tension of encounter, is that I cannot depend upon the authenticity (a complete and open involvement) of the "other" whom I encounter, so that while I may be authentic and my actions may display integrity, the situation itself may be an inauthentic one because of another's lack of integrity. Broken hearts and broken treaties both underscore such a possibility. The risks exist, and in a negative way support and substantiate the fact that one must risk one's self to achieve meaning. It is then my authenticity, under such inauthentic circumstances, which may prevent the situation from becoming totally absurd and my actions entirely meaningless. To have experienced one such betrayal is enough to substantiate both the nature of the risk and the ambiguity of the tension involved in the meaningful act. Integrity for the perspective of the self, then, would seem to imply at least two conditions: one, my willingness to respond openly to the world; and two, a synonmity between *my* belief and *my* act. Both of these conditions need further discussion.

As stated earlier, the New Humanist acknowledges that he exists in a constant state of tension with the world and that this tension is necessary for genuine encounter. The condition, however, is one which is "given" within a dynamic universe, not created; one to which I *must* respond by either encounter or withdrawal. To follow the rôle of encounter is to act with courage, for to live with tension is to live without the security of final or ultimate answers. However, to reject the role of encounter in search of security is to discover that my inauthenticity, my loss of true self-fulfillment, has robbed me of my life. So the New Humanist finds himself somewhat in the position of the man who is dieting who must convince himself that his feelings of perpetual hunger are really *good* feelings after all. Security, paradoxically enough, is to be found in the recognition and acceptance of my insecurity. Consequently my authenticity depends in part upon my continuous openness to the world with its meaning for me, and my continuous willingness to reconsider the meaningfulness of my own existence and its expression within the world. Life is never static; it is always problematic.

This leads to the second condition involved in the authenticity of the self as distinct from the situation. Authenticity (integrity) of self-expression involves a synonymity between my beliefs and thoughts and my acts. To be, to take part in a genuine encounter with the world to achieve meaning, involves a revelation of the self to world. Therefore, if I am to be intimately identified with my beliefs, then my actions and statements must accurately reveal such beliefs. I am also aware that in a world of encounter both my acts and my statements, because they do participate in a situation of tension, assume the power of definition. That is, like it or not, in terms of my encounter with the world, my actions and my statements are of equal significance with my beliefs. Thus if I am exposed in telling a lie, I cannot simply dismiss it and say, "Well, this is what I should have said." The act of the lie has "branded" me a liar. I have been defined in terms of both belief and act, and my life is inauthentic for me and absurd for a world which can no longer understand me. The New Humanist would want it clearly understood at this point that a lie is not to be considered as the intentional denial of "facts," nor the intentional violation of the moral code of a fixed world view, but as the intentional denial of truth.

In terms of the above synonymity, truth can only be considered an expression of authenticity. But truth for the New

Humanist, as Heidegger argues, is not an abstract principle, a Platonic universal, nor is it some obtainable verification of the factualness of reality. Truth for the New Humanist must be thought of as the faithful expression of one's being, one's total self, in terms of care and resolve within the world— whether this occurs in act or in statement. Thus the husband, at the suggestion of the physician, may not tell his wife of her terminal cancer and yet be telling the truth. By withholding the information or by substituting other information, he may be faithfully expressing his and the physician's belief that she would be unable to cope with such a verdict and that he must, out of love, bear it for her. On the other hand, it is quite conceivable that the converse might be truth. It could be that to withhold such information would be to enact a lie, to be unfaithful to a stronger, more secure person. For the New Humanist authenticity and truth have to do with *Being* and its expression, not with fact and its proper recording. Surely some support for this claim can be found in the common, though often disturbed, acceptance of the so-called white lie, or in the lack of guilt feelings when we believe that a lie, e.g., in terms of health, was justifiable. For the New Humanist, *Being* takes priority over "knowing." Again the element of risk recurs, but again one notes that meaning is only achieved at the price of risk. Authenticity in all its forms can only express itself under constant tension and possibility of inauthenticity.

Authenticity is thus an expression of my being-in-the-world-here-and-now. My life is such that my humanity, my value as a person, is not at stake; only my integrity as that person is continuously in question. This integrity as a person involves my living responsively in a world in which meaning is created and experienced through such responsibility, through my encounter with the world. This creative encounter is that which gives power, character, and expression to my life, and its exercise with integrity enables me to claim authenticity of *Being*. Such integrity involves my openness to the world, my total responsiveness to that world, and a consistency of self-expression which is the truthfulness of *Being*. Authenticity is thus the responsive and responsible expression of *Being*-in-the-world-here-and-now.

The second emphasis of the New Humanism is the expression of freedom. In a technological age in which the tyranny of method and form is combined with the unlimited availability of mass-produced, qualitatively-limited goods, and the System in all its forms has become a mandatory expression of the Establishment, the meaning of freedom has become an issue of crucial importance. The authenticity which the New Humanists seek to establish is grounded in the expression of freedom.

But freedom for the New Humanist should not be understood as simply the existential precondition of authenticity, though it does perform that function. Nor is freedom considered to be the necessary concomitant of *Being* as air, for example, is necessary for physical existence. Rather, freedom must be understood as an integral aspect of life itself, or more accurately, of *Being* itself. Thus, if one is truly to understand freedom, one must describe it in terms of *Being*.

Being as Heidegger argues is "isness;" it is "existence;" it is, in the case of man, "self-awareness." But it is at this point that the evidence of ambiguity and paradox enter in, and language is strained in an effort to carry exact meaning. Self-awareness, as an act of *Being*, carries with it, as Buber suggests, an awareness of others—both people and things. But awareness is not common identity. I can only know *my* "self" in so far as I am able to distinguish it from the other selves and expressions of *Being* about me. Were this not true there would be no need for me to employ the possessive pronoun "my." The implications of such an observation are important not only in the understanding of *Being* but in the understanding of *Being*'s expression in freedom.

Self-awareness and the coincident other-awareness mean that my identity as a person involves a limitation of my *Being*, as well as the limitation of the *Being* of others. That is, I can actually say that I experience both a continuity of *Being* and a discontinuity, i.e., a physical and psychical limitation, of *Being* in my relationship to the world. I may be in-the-world-here-and-now, but such an identifying statement does not mean that I am totally and indistinguishably at one with that world-here-and-now. I am, but I am not, at one with the reader of this book, and I am even less at one with the physical book itself. Though all three—you, the book, and myself —participate in a common expression of *Being* and, for that matter, being- here-and-now, we are also, in terms of identity, discontinuous. At this point of discontinuity identity involves limitation, i.e., *Non-being*.

On the other hand, identity likewise involves "extension." The fact that I *can* distinguish myself from you and from the book, and that such a distinction is both a qualitative and quantitative one, indicates that in some way the expression of *Being* or "isness" gives us a common identity, a mutuality-in-*Being*, which unites us in the ground of our uniqueness. We get the point when the rough voice says: "Me Tarzan, you Jane." The distinction between this understanding of the human condition and Hegel's "similarity involved in difference" is precisely the issue of freedom. The uniqueness of the New Humanist's ontological expression of *Being* is truly, time-fully new; it is not simply the new configuration of an organically structured dialectic. For the New Humanist, identity is an act of creation, not accommodation.

It is likewise true, as the discussion of Buber in Chapter III suggests, that it is through my creative encounter with other human beings that I develop and mature into the person that I am. This is true, to a lesser extent (at least qualitatively), with the objective world with which I also interact. Thus, for the New Humanist, my *Being* can only be understood in terms of an organic, relational world in which both the limitation of *Non-being* and the extension of *Being* are simultaneously involved. It is the possibility of self-expression, within such a relational context, which is understood as freedom.

The most immediate and intimate awareness of freedom as *Being's* self-expression is experienced within the individual consciousness which, while preoccupied with itself, finds that it cannot escape the "other." What I am referring to is commonly called the act of self-transcendence. Here self-awareness transcends identity in a mysterious way; the knower is not the known self, nor can the knower ever be known; and yet, the knower is intimately aware that what he is conscious of is himself. The spontaneous self (knower) is aware of the conditional self (known), and as a result, self-identity participates in its own limitation and extension, its own discontinuousness and organic relationship. Is not such self-transcendence implicit in the experience of judgment which we continuously exercise on our own thought and work and in our consequent resolution to improve? Freedom is the spontaneous expression of *Being* in a relational context.

It is only the curtailment or prohibition of such self-expression that makes us "self-conscious" about this particular act of *Being*, much like the experience of sickness makes us aware of the condition of health. Freedom, therefore, is not really a special or distinct characteristic of *Being*, it is more a term for identifying the fundamental expression or dimension of *Being*. The denial of this expression is actually the result of inauthenticity within myself (e.g., cowardice or pretense) or with my encounter with the world (e.g., political inactivism or tyranny). The very fact that "freedom," as commonly used, is a correlative term for such words as "determinism," "containment," or "prohibition," would support the above contention that freedom is really nothing other than *Being's* act of self-expression.

Freedom, as a dimension of *Being*, only becomes paradoxical when it is considered as "something" extraneous to *Being* itself, as that which is imposed upon or added to *Being* rather than integral to it. Consequently the New Humanism would reject Sartre's notion that man is "condemned to be free." Any sense of condemnation would imply a condition imposed upon *Being* rather than a condition expressive of *Being*. On the other hand, the New Humanism would accept the less dramatic existentialist assertion that we are not free not to choose. Here the negation implies internal authority, an expression of *Being* in terms of its own nature, not an imposition from without.

Freedom, of course, is the presupposition of my authentic relationship to the world. Without freedom the tension which exists between myself and the world would not characterize personal encounters mentioned earlier in this chapter. Rather such tension would be resolved through the mechanical process of measurement, e.g., I am forceful enough, economically, to impose my will in *this* situation, but I find that I am totally overpowered in *that* situation. Thus my authenticity would be reduced to the endless and personally meaningless balancing of some intricately structured system. It is also true that without the condition and exercise of freedom there could be no creative encounter as the expression of personal uniqueness and authenticity. The possibilities of personal expression would already be prefigured by the established limitations of the participants. Such encounters would provide a calculus for the computer not the context for creation. The welter of mechanical testing services take us far enough along this road already.

At this point it would be well to consider the nature of choice which has so often been identified with the expression of freedom. For the New Humanist the freedom identified with choice is best understood as the exercise of authentic encounter in which I am involved with the world. The determination of whether to follow one course of action or another, or to believe one idea or another, is really a matter of my integrity in self-expression. Such action is singled out for attention when, as we noted before, my self-expression is prohibited or forcibly curtailed. The power behind the argument for "freedom of choice" is not the power of some abstract principle or inalienable right, but rather the power of *Being* to express itself, to be.

When choice is considered in political and social affairs —the right to vote, the right to choose where I want to live— one does not have a new "truth" introduced, a new condition of *Being*. Rather such freedom is the extension of the power of *Being* expressing itself in its organic or corporate dimension. It is the corporate analogue of the spontaneity and limitation which interact in the identity of individuals. So it is that one considers instigating political reform or revolt, *not* when one's candidate loses an election, *but* when the election itself is denied, or the candidates are arbitrarily imposed upon the electorate. Under the conditions of forcible restriction, one raises the cry of freedom—not for its own sake but for the sake of the identity, the character, the meaning of the community whose self-expression has been denied.

Freedom as a dimension of *Being* up to this point has only been discussed in the general terms of self-expression and community expression, but there is a more specific reference than these generalizations. For the New Humanist, that dimension of *Being* most directly involved in self-expression is creativity. Perhaps it is for this reason that the avantgarde in the search for the New Morality is to be found more in the arts than in professional philosophy or theology or politics.

For the New Humanist, to be is to express oneself meaningfully in the world which one responsibly encounters. As noted earlier, such encounter, open and responsive, is the ground of all meaning and meaningful *Being*. Thus, when the encounter is authentic and not improperly inhibited, the result is a unique, thoughtful, imaginative, and therefore a new expression of *Being*—a creation. In this same way, the artist in his contact with the world creates: it is an impression and an expression of meaning. This is true even in the very "subjective" expression of meaning simply in terms of line, color, and space. Yet in each case, the creation is an expression of his *Being*, his identity. This is likewise true in the more general use of the term "create," in the relationship between people. The authentic encounter produces a friendship which is unique, meaningful, responsible, and new and, as such, instrumental in the creation of identity. Unique self-expression emerges from the creative act, which is what freedom is all about.

Albert Camus as "artist" and New Humanist wrote of this correlation in *Resistance, Rebellion, and Death*:

The aim of art, the aim of a life can only be to increase the sum of freedom and responsibility to be found in every man and in the world. It cannot, under any circumstances, be to reduce or suppress that freedom, even temporarily. . . . On the contrary, there is not a single true work of art that has not in the end added to the inner freedom of each person who has known and loved it.[6]

The third of the central characteristics of the New Humanism is that of affirmation. Basically affirmation involves my rational response to *Being*, to my existence or "isness" as potentially self-expressive. Such an affirmation is grounded in the polar relation which exists between *Being* and *Non-being*, existence and nonexistence; and the tension within this polarity makes a continuous confirmation of my personal existence necessary. But this affirmation of the New Humanism is more than the sheer choice between life and death; it is likewise more positive than an act of *mere* acceptance. To understand affirmation as the positive rational response to *Being*, one must again consider *Being* itself.

As Heidegger indicates, *Being* is not simply a definitional or "logical" category relative to its polar category *Non-being*. *Being* involves me in its character so that my self-expression participates in and is expressive of that character. My life is more than *am*; it carries the revelational force of *I am*. Consequently my affirmation in terms of my *Being* is more than sheer or simple "hereness;" it is an awareness of my involvement with power. This affirmation in terms of power expresses itself in a variety of ways. It is, perhaps first of all, the power to create. It is my ability and "nature" to interpret, to organize, and accordingly to respond to the world as I am engaged with it, which re-emphasizes that meaning emerges from encounter. I usually discern quickly enough that this "world" which I have "created" is inconsistent with further experience or is inadequate to explain past experience examined more closely. Consequently I must recreate my world by reinterpreting and reorganizing my experience—but in this action I am impressed by the fact that the process involved is again a creative one.

The recognition is always present that I again may be inadequate in my comprehension of experience and that what I call "reality" must be reassessed. Yet it is important to recognize that such a process is never merely the response to some ultimate truth standard or some ultimate organic universal which "corrects" my vision and understanding. Rather the power of creation always involves me in the risk of the radically new, and because I am a *Being* of finitude and time, the radically incomplete. For similar reasons such creativity is a repudiation of any thoroughgoing determinism. The two conditions are simply antithetical. Because of its radical uniqueness and radical incompleteness, creativity is a denial of the absoluteness or ultimacy of any specific external judgment whether it be by the world, man, or God. Thus the conclusion must be that my power to create is the continuous affirmation of my life in terms of my perception, my reason, my emotion, my imagination, my intuition—in point of fact, my total self in encounter with the world. Thus I do not simply face the world; rather, I find myself engaging a world for which I am creatively, albeit only partially, responsible. Such ambiguity is involved in the act of affirmation. When I refuse this responsibility *of Being*, my world becomes chaotic, and reaction replaces affirmation. When such a reaction response becomes chronic, we say that the person is neurotic or psychopathic. The terror and/or confusion of such a state is not the loss of creativity but the loss of personal control. The creative process continues, and its power is such that it can destroy us as science, fact or fiction, loves to remind us. As noted before, affirmation of the world involves risk.

But what of that specialized creativity we attribute to writers and painters, musicians and architects? What we call "creative" in this context is the extraordinary power some men have to express objectively the subjective configurations of their "created" world. The fact that we as laymen can respond to such creative expressions is indicative of the fact that we, too, participate in that creative process, and, though we do not possess the gift of their expressive excellence, we are led to respond with creative understanding. Perhaps this gift of understanding is why we so often respond with indebtedness to a writer by saying, "That's what I've always thought, but I have never been able to put it into words before!" Albert

Camus in *Resistance, Rebellion, and Death* again lends support:

The aim of art is not to legislate or to reign supreme, but rather to understand first of all. Sometimes it does reign supreme, as a result of understanding. But no work of genius has ever been based on hatred and contempt. This is why the artist, at the end of his slow advance, absolves instead of condemning. Instead of being a judge, he is a justifier. He is the perpetual advocate of the living creature, because it is alive. He truly argues for love of one's neighbor and not for that love of the remote stranger which debases contemporary humanism until it becomes the catechism of the law court. Instead, the great work eventually confounds all judges. With it the artist simultaneously pays homage to the loftiest figure of mankind and bows down before the worst of criminals.[7]

Affirmation as a sense of power is also experienced in our ability to withstand adversity, to endure, as Faulkner so eloquently described it in his acceptance of the Nobel Prize for Literature in 1949.

I decline to accept the end of man. It is easy enough to say that man is immortal simply because he will endure; that when the last ding-dong of doom has clanged and faded from the last worthless rock hanging tideless in the last red and dying evening, that even then there will still be one more sound: that of his puny inexhaustible voice, still talking. I refuse to accept this. I believe that man will not merely endure: he will prevail. He is immortal, not because he alone among creatures has an inexhaustible voice, but because he has a soul, a spirit capable of compassion and sacrifice and endurance. The poet's, the writer's, duty is to write about these things. It is his privilege to help man endure by lifting his heart, by reminding him of the courage and honor and hope and pride and compassion and pity and sacrifice which have been the glory of his past. The poet's voice need not merely be the record of man, it can be one of the props, the pillars to help him endure and prevail.[8]

Our power to withstand is more than our ability to face adversity; it is finally the power to confront the basic anxieties of life, the most fundamental of which is death. To know that we are to die, to have that fact dramatically brought home to us each day in terms of the death of others, and yet to plan, to prepare, to educate, and even to sacrifice, all point to the power of affirmation expressed in the act of living itself. It is not simply a balance of positive forces and negative forces, good times and bad times; it is rather the power of the self to assert its own meaning and to affirm its own meaningfulness in spite of the forces that threaten its cultural effectiveness or psychospiritual health, and that promise its physical demise.

Affirmation as a sense of power is also found in our ability to evaluate. We are not simply the victims of perception or experience, passive recorders or computers of events as they occur. We judge, we assess, we emphasize, we depreciate, and we discuss events and experiences in which we participate, and by such an evaluation we not only control our creative responsiveness but also condition that responsiveness for the future. The power of such evaluation is seen negatively in the inordinate exercise of the evaluation process untempered by the creative act of re-evaluation, reinterpretation—in the set or prejudiced mind; "No use talking to me; I know what I believe." Under such conditions, we impose a structure upon the world which is not the result of our continuous interaction with it but is our relative, individualized configuration which we have unwarrantedly absolutized. Such absolutizing cannot help distort our understanding of life, for it attempts to fix and make permanent that which by its nature is changing, relative, incomplete, and creative.

Another expression of power which contributes to the New Humanist's affirmation of life is our ability to control. Human existence is simply not one great hazardous event after another; man has learned that he is not totally helpless in the presence of an imposing impersonal, if not hostile, physical world, in the presence of great social and economic forces, and in the face of his own ignorance and estrangement. Man is doing remarkable things: he is learning to control the energy of the sun; he is exploring outer space; he is controlling or curtailing the effects of most diseases; he anticipates controlling even the weather. By his rational use of money, goods, and services he can rehabilitate nations, provide hope for underprivileged societies, and stabilize the economies of the world. Through education he has learned the patterns of human behavior so that he can not only influence the behavior of others but also comprehend his own.

Such controls in the hands of man are awesome expressions of power. As a matter of fact, such power is so awesome that we arbitrarily impose limits upon nations, societies, and individuals so that excessive control will not be irresponsibly exercised or pass into the hands of too few. As nations we are concerned about the controlled use of atomic energy; as industrial societies we are moving slowly toward common markets which impose mutual controls; as individuals we are learning to inhibit that expression of self which becomes destructive for the community in which we live. Of course risk is again involved. The line between control and unwarranted imposition is a hard line to draw, yet we do recognize the difference between the two and are obliged by our search for authenticity to make the distinction. Ambiguity is always risk.

All of the above—the power to create, to withstand, to evaluate, and to control—can be summed up in the power *to be*. The experience of my *Being*, my existing, which is expressive of all of the above powers, is the affirmation about which the New Humanism speaks. Such powers are constructive, affirming *my Being* in its encounter with the *Being* of others and the world; such powers are mine, providing for me a unique expression of my identity; such powers are indestructible at least to the point of death. *To be* is to say *yes* to the world—and for the world.

In addition to affirmation being understood in terms of these general expressions of power, the affirmation of the New Humanism must be understood more specifically as an assertion of reason itself. This affirmation-through-reason is not simply the recovery of eighteenth-century Rationalism which arrogantly assumed the supremacy of reason in the quest of knowledge and truth; the rationalism of the New Humanism is grounded in the historical events of the last eight decades and tempered by the psychological and philosophical revolution of the nineteenth and twentieth centuries. Psychology, since the time of Freud, has demonstrated to us that much of our reasoning is really rationalization, a justification of an idea or position for which or to which there has already been an emotional commitment. While granting this insight, the New Humanist has also observed that the obtaining, understanding, and communicating of such an insight depends directly upon the power of reason. Thus what emerges from such a tempering process is a new and more comprehensive understanding of reason. Reason, while necessary, cannot supply its own necessity or provide its own verification. It is, in short, ambiguous.

The process of reason's refinement is also furthered by the insights of existentialist philosophy which remind man that he cannot understand himself by objective analysis, for he is first and foremost a "subjective" being. This means that man, in terms of his own reality, must take into account his moods, his feelings, his intuitions, his imaginings, as well as his reason. Man is not only rational, he is "irrational" as well. Again, the ambiguity of reason emerges. Reason is not worthless; it has simply become apparent that the eighteenth-century definition of reason is an inadequate one; or, holding to that definition of reason as the ratiocinative functioning of the mind, we see that understanding is a greater, more complex experience than the "logical" functioning of the brain. Thus these contributions by the existentialists have freed the New Humanists to speak in terms of the Self, not by excluding reason but by redefining it in terms of its correlation with other forms of perception, expression, and response mentioned above. The Self is not merely rational or "irrational"; it is suprarational. Again it should be noted that poverty of language forces us to use the term "rational" here in terms of its traditional "logical" function.

The third tradition which has contributed to the New Humanist's understanding of reason is that of traditional British empiricism. Empiricism was not content to let reason be self-sufficient as the source of knowledge but insisted upon the primacy of experience, experimentation, and even feeling. Under such strictures, it is the function of reason to organize, coordinate, and interpret the data provided by such experience and experimentation. The contemporary American movement of logical empiricism was a refinement of this argument but carried the critique to such an extreme that it soon could not even talk of reason *per se* but rather of language sets or language systems. While the New Humanism finds little hope or help in these extreme forms of empiricism, it is instructed by the more moderate form. The quest is for understanding, not information.

Reason, while it does express itself in definite patterns and forms must at the same time incorporate that which is indefinite, experimental, transitional, and "nonrational." Again, as with the Freudian and existentialist critiques, reason emerges as redefined, or as that function of the Self which orders experience within the greater ambiguities of existence. In each case, however, reason reappears as an affirmative and creative factor in the understanding of the world and of one's self. The encounter with a meaningful world, a world in which emotion, self, and sense perception are correlated (though not fixed) and communicated (though not imposed), provides the New Humanist with his affirmation-through-reason.

The affirmation of the New Humanism is clearly an expression of a sophisticated realism rather than a naive idealism. In his search for authenticity, in his exercise of freedom, and in keeping with his affirmation the New Humanist is capable and willing to assume responsibility for life. Such a perspective is free of what he must consider hypocritical value norms or irrelevant historical precedents and is post-existential in its rejection of despair, tragedy, and absurdity as the finalities of human existence. Albert Camus said: "The absurd is born of this confrontation between human need and the unreasonable silence of the world." The New Humanist seems to be saying: "What absurdity there is is born born of the confrontation between human need and the irrational, inauthentic silence of men!" Both the responsibility and the risk are ours.

five: Ambiguity

THE POWER and thrust of the search for the New Humanism is evident in the attempts of artists, philosophers, and theologians to transcend the dualisms of traditional Western metaphysics and to avoid the anthropomorphic excesses of traditional Hebraic thought. The New Humanists no more believe life to be governed by man's knowledge of the Absolute than they believe it to be governed by a patriarchal tribal God. Rather, it is the hope of the New Humanists to transform the insights of each of these heritages: the ability of man to abstract and utilize his reasoning capacity, which led to the development of Western science and the scientific method, should not be ignored or deprecated; and the need for man to understand his indebtedness to and, at the same time, his creation of history should not be underestimated.

The transformation of traditions is effected by the New Humanist's insistence upon *Being* (in the time-full, ontological sense) as the ground for understanding man's thought and action, his knowing and doing. A few examples of transformation will, perhaps, clarify the issue.

Moral sensitivity is not, on the one hand, a matter of a Platonic intellectual perception of the Good, the Stoic attainment of harmony with Nature, or the medieval beatific vision of God; nor is it, on the other hand, a matter of ritual purity, an irrational fidelity to tradition, or a scriptural legalism. For the New Humanism, moral sensitivity is effected by a response to *Being* rather than a response to rule or form. Consequently it is continuously being interpreted and expressed in keeping with personal responsibility to myself and others (though there is no absolute dichotomy here in terms of *Being*). For example, one's fidelity in marriage is not occasioned by a belief in the infallibility of the laws of the State, nor by a belief in the infallibility of a religious liturgy, nor by any absolute "Thou shalt not. . . ." Fidelity is the expression of commitment within the *I-Thou* relation of love, the acknowledgment of a primary orientation toward another which is so complete and so consuming that it cannot admit an equal, a second. For those who express a religious commitment, i.e., marriage as a sacrament or religious act, the relationship may assume an even greater meaning with overtones not evident in the secular understanding of *I-Thou* relation, but that does not change the character of that relation. It remains the same for secular and sacred expression.

The experience of evil could be another example of this transformation of tradition. If evil can be defined as that force which is willfully harmful or destructive of life (as opposed to accidentally or impersonally harmful), then evil cannot be understood as the necessity of cultural determinism ("I grew up during the depression"), fate ("my number was up"), chance ("that's the way the cookie crumbled"), or simply the lack of adequate knowledge in me or in another;

nor can it be understood as the breaking of laws, or the ignoring of custom. Evil for the New Humanism is more like the early Greek notion of *hubris* as arrogance and/or willful, irresponsible violence, and the prophetic notion of sin as apostasy, as rebellion against God. Both of these notions carry with them the willful isolation of self from the ground of *Being* and the idolatrous (secular and sacred) assumption of the power of *Being* itself. Thus, for the New Humanism any act of mine is evil which destroys authenticity in myself or denies it to or in another. Racial prejudice, which ghettos another because of the color of his skin is not only inauthentic, it is evil. Evil is the betrayal of *Being*. Again it can be said that those of a religious persuasion may find overtones in evil of an alienation, a loss of identity and authenticity not apparent in the secular perspective; but, again it must be noted that the effective character of evil is the same in each case.

One last example of the transformation of tradition which occurs in the New Humanism could be its adherents' concept of the nature of truth. Truth is not a Platonic metaphysical reality which the mind can perceive through reason, or by the proper exercise of the rules of logic, or as the comprehension of "all that is"; nor is truth revelation in the form of propositional statements of God, the Ten Commandments, or Scripture. Truth, as noted in Chapter III, is the evident expression of my authenticity of *Being*; it is the faithful expression of myself to others in terms of the nature of the context in which I find myself. The key phrase here is "nature of the context." Such a "nature" is understood to mean the degree of my open and free participation in the *I-Thou* encounter. The truth, then, is that which is appropriate to the nature of my immediate relationship judged by the degree of openness experienced. If my relationship is *I-It,* then the truth carries with it the nature of an objective judgment. For example, a clerk in a store says to me: "How are you?" My response tends to be: "I am fine, thank you." Such a response is true to the nature of the context, even though to a good friend I might have responded: "Not too bad, but my ulcer has been acting up lately." The clerk in the store—in the context of *I-It*—is no more interested in my ulcer than I am in telling him, but such is not true of my friend who, I trust, is genuinely concerned about me and who would be offended by a superficial answer. My response to the clerk is appropriate, for if I told him what I would tell a friend he would be embarrassed or perhaps even annoyed. To know is to be involved, but such involvement is part of the *I-Thou* relation, not the *I-It*.

Again, one can say that for those who express a religious commitment, there may be overtones and obligations not experienced by the secular man, e.g., the *I-Thou* relation with God may seem to require that I be ready to express myself openly to all men in all situations. The truth under such circumstances is defined by my relationship to God, which governs all other relationships. To know the truth, then, is really to be the truth in relationship to God, and this is the "knowledge" which sets one free for all other relationships.

All of these examples show that the New Humanism is convinced that there is no absolute code of Goodness (Wisdom, Justice, Temperance, Courage) or divine Law (Ten Commandments, Sermon on the Mount) which can take from me the necessity of making the moral decisions for which I am responsible. Nor is there any verifiable End (Happiness, Goodness) or Kingdom (Heaven, Hell) whose function it is to prescribe my acts. In every situation in which I am confronted by choice, I must respond in terms of my authenticity. My authenticity as described earlier is my openness to *Being*. It emerges out of the act of engagement for which there is no objective standard or pre-existent law. To live authentically, therefore, is to live in risk, in tension, in the ambiguities constructed by the intricate web of possibilities, probabilities, and actualities.

The characteristic mark of this New Humanism which arises out of time-full *Being* is ambiguity, and it is to this concept that we should now turn our attention. William Empson, who has discussed "ambiguity" at length in *Seven Types of Ambiguity*, gives the literary scope of ambiguity's use, e.g., as paradox, contradiction, multimeaning, etc., but the nature of *ambiguity as limitation* is not discussed. It is in this sense that ambiguity is important to the New Humanism.

In the expression of the three characteristics of the New Humanism we have discussed—authenticity, freedom, and affirmation—ambiguity assumes a central role. The limitation and uncertainty which I experienced in these expressions of my *Being* are not simply the limitations of ignorance or error which could be corrected by further study; they are rather the limitations of the very nature of my *Being*. To be authentic I must participate in an act of engagement (*I-Thou*) with another. The very fact of that act is witness to the fundamental nature of these limitations. The validity and completeness of that act depend upon the openness with which *I* and my *Thou* respond to each other. I can only know as much of him as he permits me to know (and vice versa), and every human relationship is subject to such limitation. Martin Buber insists that the true *I-Thou* relationship has no limits, no bounds, but this is really the limitlessness which exists within the confines of the relationship, somewhat analogous to the limitless number of divisions or points I can mathematically make on any specified line.

Even more telling, perhaps, than this limitation in relationship is the fact that I cannot communicate everything about myself to another even if I want to; I simply find that

I am, finally, a mystery to myself. This is in part true because of the fact that I change in time: I get new ideas, new insights, new doubts; I create new things, new images, new symbols; I respond (and therefore change) because of new experiences, new loves, new fears. From one moment to the next there is no guarantee that I will remain unchanged. But self-knowledge is, in final analysis, simply impossible if for no other reason than that existence, because it is in time, simply prohibits my ever "knowing" the knower, i.e., I am never aware of true self-awareness. The very ambiguity of this statement is perhaps proof enough of limitation.

There is a limitation in *Being* which is the limitation of knowing. Even those who have been happily and contentedly married over a long period of time still find that elusive mystery of ambiguity, that lack of final knowledge, evident in the relationship. Contrariwise such "ambiguity" explains why some couples seemingly happy, surrounded by children, can get a divorce after twenty years of marriage. There is no guarantee, for times change and so do we.

Authenticity also involves thoughts, statements, and acts which are appropriate to a given context, not to an absolute standard or law, which again expresses the limitation of ambiguity, i.e., laws deemed suitable for one cultural condition or time may be totally inadequate in another. America's "Sunday Closing Laws" are a good example. As the nation becomes multireligious, we are finding it inappropriate to force Jews, Seventh Day Adventists, etc. to observe the Christian custom. There is nothing sacred about such laws, and they should be changed to meet the needs of the context.

This same sort of ambiguity is germane for more of life than just social situations. Education itself can only thrive in an atmosphere of ambiguity. To think that I have all the answers, to think that I know all there is to know in any given discipline is to stifle curiosity, interest, and activity. All education, including the most exact sciences, assumes that new knowledge is available, that old ways are inadequate, that more comprehension is possible. The genuine excitement of education comes in its promise of endless ambiguity. The minute learning becomes final, it becomes ideological, and that sounds the death knell for scholarship, advancement of knowledge, and truth-in-relation. This the Russians soon discovered when Lysenko's theories on heredity became tenets of a political expression. Educational life cannot abide finality.

Nor can religious life abide absolutism or finality. When religious belief becomes set in dogmas which attempt to confine and define it, "belief" in its time-full, verbal significance (as Heidegger observed about *Being*) is relegated to the sterility of a fixed, static noun. Belief is the expression of free association of man and his God. This belief, even when one claims that it is a response to the initiating act of God Himself, is still "belief" and not final knowledge. It is still ambiguous; it is still an act of will, of imagination, of trust on the part of the believer. Belief exists under conditions which make public knowledge impossible and private knowledge unverifiable—even for the believer himself. Thus, when such belief, describing or denoting the relationship of man to God, becomes explicit in a creed or dogma which is declared final, it has ceased to be belief and has become idolatry.

This is one of the dangers about which existentialist theologians and death-of-God proponents have been warning us. These contemporary thinkers are seriously trying to avoid the oppressive conformity of an outmoded orthodox cosmology which, they maintain, restricts man's creativity, ignores his responsibility, and destroys his freedom to be. To subject man, in the name of religion, to categories of thought which no longer have the power to point beyond themselves or to involve man religiously, is, for God's sake, idolatry. The fact that such "idolatry" is irrelevant for contemporary man is certainly implicit in such criticism. Whether destructive or constructive, what these theologians are attempting to do is to shock us out of our nonreligion into the act or commitment of faith which must be free, personal, authetic, and holy.

But contemporary theologians are not the first to offer such advice. It is the same terrifyingly attractive lure of religious finality about which we have been warned in Scripture from God's ambiguous "response" to Moses' request for His name: "I am who I am," to Jesus' words of caution to those who lived in Bethsaida-and-about: "No one knows the Son except the Father, and no one knows the Father except the Son."[1] Religious finality is the cardinal temptation by that snake in Eden: "You will be like God, knowing good and evil."[2] Finality is the death of reason and religion; ambiguity is the possibility of life.

Of course this means risk and tension, but reality as we have discovered is always risk and tension. This is the mark of ambiguity. It is true that in some situations, e.g., war, the risks and hazards are more dramatic, more crucial, than secretarial work; but the tensions of ambiguity are evident in each. The limitations of the unknown and unknowable affect each life. It is for this reason that the word "authenticity" is used by the New Humanist. If knowledge of identity and character were final or absolute or measurable, then "right" Being or "correct" Being would be far more suitable than "authentic" Being. "Authentic" carries with it the connotation of dynamism, of change, of context, of appropriateness; not of finality. It suggests reciprocity, not conformity.

Freedom is another form of ambiguous expression. Freedom, as indicated earlier, is the ground for my creative encounter with the world. Both words, "creative" and "encounter," are involved in ambiguity and need to be considered here. "Creative" implies something new, unique, unknown; it is not something discovered as already pre-existing. If life were somehow programmed in cause-effect dimensions, or if life were predetermined by some divine power, then there would be no need for such a word as "create"; things would evolve, emerge, or be discovered. The experience of the artist involved in creative arts would have to be totally other than it seems to him, for he believes that his work of art is new, is a unique expression of himself or his understanding of the world. Such determinism would also affect those of us who can only "appreciate" art, not create it. When we interpret a work of art we realize the ambiguity involved. Even as dilettantes we are most indignant when some callow critic informs us that he and he alone can give us *the* interpretation of a painting, a piece of music, a poem. If no one else will reprimand him, the artist himself will. With the possible exception of commercial art, when the purpose is merely denotative, T. S. Eliot's instruction holds: a poem can only mean what it means to the reader; there is no right-reading. This should not suggest, of course, that there is no direction or context. It simply means that there is no denotation which must be necessarily ascertained. Ambiguity is the life-blood of all artistic creation.

One further note on the word "creative" as used in the phrase "creative encounter." If that encounter is with another person, then, as Buber has argued, the result is new and unique, and the effect on the persons involved is new and unique. It is not like the mixing of chemicals where the results can be mathematically anticipated and the effects reproduced at will. The true encounter takes place in ambiguity. I cannot predict the results of any specific encounter, as anyone knows who has tried to introduce two of his "very close friends" to each other. There is apt to be an embarrassing awkwardness after the pleasantries are over. Those young people who have depended upon the computer for dates know all too well that the factors of love involve subtleties far too ambiguous to program on an I.B.M. "120."

The spontaneity of freedom is likewise indicative of an unstructured and therefore ambiguous context. The totally calculated act, the determined act, if these represent strictures other than the spontaneous determination of my own being, deny any real concept of freedom. The word "spontaneous" implies that we are not limited by some tyranny of time, some absolute historical determination which reduces meaningfulness in time to measure by time. Spontaneity implies that each moment is new, present for me with possibilities which demand my encounter and decision. I may decide in terms of my memory of the past or in terms of my anticipation of the future; more likely, however, I shall try to decide in terms of both of these factors plus a third-and-primary one, my immediate context: thoughts, desires, pressures, etc. The meaningfulness of *Being*-here-and-now and the ambiguous context of my pending death focus attention on the here-and-now.

This consideration of the spontaneity of freedom, however, brings us to the heart of what the New Humanist calls "freedom" and that is spontaneous self-expression. To be is to be open to the future, to choose in terms of who I am, not just what I know. Dostoevsky well understood the ambiguity of this. In *Notes from the Underground* he writes:

Reason only knows what it has succeeded in learning . . . and human nature acts as a whole, with everything that is in it, consciously or unconsciously, and even if it goes wrong, it lives. . . . There is one case, one only, when man may consciously, purposely, desire what is injurious to himself, what is stupid, very stupid—simply in order to have the right to desire for himself even what is very stupid and not to be bound by an obligation to desire only what is sensible. Of course, this very stupid thing, this caprice of ours, may be in reality . . . more advantageous for us than anything else on earth. . . .—for in any circumstances it preserves for us what is most precious and most important—that is, our personality, our individuality.[3]

One can surmise that Dostoevsky is arguing for a "larger rationality," which may be true, but even this larger rationality is limited so that my total response is one of considered appropriateness not behavioral determinism. This is a response in freedom, which does not preclude the possibility of other appropriate responses in the same context. Anytime we are in the position of expressing gratitude (letter? words? gift?) we face the ambiguity of freedom. To always follow the dictates of conventional etiquette may turn out to be a denial of gratitude.

The New Humanist notion of affirmation is likewise an expression of ambiguity. We do not "confirm" life, as though we could place our stamp of approval on the master plan; we can only respond to that which we do know and experience. We can make an affirmation only in terms of *now*, based upon the past and in anticipation of the future. But even here ambiguity is evident. Our understanding of the past may alter, e.g., a war which seemed just in the beginning may turn out to be totally unjust; our understanding of the future must always take into consideration the fact of death about which we know nothing other than its physical occurrence. For those who have a religious conviction that some form of life and justice persist beyond death, the ambiguity of belief is as evident and limiting as the ambiguity of death is to the secularist. Affirmation is my "Yes" to a context which is constantly being threatened by my "No." My rational response to *Being* is always one conditioned by freedom and authenticity. *Being* gives no guarantee; it simply *is*. Because it *is*, my response is governed by ambiguity.

Along with the affirmation of reason, the New Humanist

finds affirmation in the awareness of power, but here, again, ambiguity is evident. The power of which I am aware is my limited ability to act but, at the same time, my complete inability to sustain myself in such action. I cannot will myself into the future, for I have no control over time or *Being*; I cannot will my death, for though I can stop bodily processes by suicide, I have no idea of what death (other than physical cessation) really means. Thus the power which I experience —the power to create, to withstand adversity, to evaluate, to control, to be—is my real but limited power of self-expression here-and-now, which any number of other forces or powers can cancel in a moment. This power to cancel does not negate my affirmation but only marks its ambiguous, limited nature.

Support for this understanding of ambiguity is evident in contributions of the artists, musicians, and writers whose rôle in the development of the New Humanism we have already discussed. The limitation which marks such ambiguity is evident in the responsible action of both the artist and the public. For the artist it is the limitation in presentation; for the public it is the limitation of interpretation. But this is not to imply that either the creative act or the creative appreciation suffers loss of meaning; rather such ambiguity simply describes the nature of human expression and perception.

The artist's creation, while it does represent a form of completeness, is nevertheless only part of his continuing awareness of his multidimensional world. What he has expressed—himself—must be expressed again in a continuously changing context. Finley Eversole states: "The courage of the contemporary artist is essentially a courage of existence, of facing of the abyss by one who lives by the conviction of his own finitude."[4] Such conviction, such affirmation, is the inherent ambiguity in the life and work of the artist.

The artist Rico Lebrun seems to be particularly aware of the tension of ambiguity in artistic endeavor:

This is my curse, that when I see certain finished statements they seem to have come too soon to a finish, which *is* finish, because it avoids bloody combat and concentrates on execution. Too soon, too soon, too good, too ready, lacking the intake of breath between one natal or parturient spasm and another; when the body-mind rocks bewildered asking for mercy between one stage of "finish" and another.[5]

But the tension of ambiguity does not end with the artist. Because he is acutely aware of his own limitation, he is equally aware of the limitations of his public and their ability to "understand" him. Igor Stravinsky says: "Music should be transmitted and not interpreted, because interpretation reveals the personality of the interpreter rather than that of the author, and who can guarantee that such an executant will reflect the author's vision without distortion?"[6] Pablo Picasso apparently agrees: "Everyone wants to understand art. Why not try to understand the song of a bird? One loves the night flowers, everything around one, without trying to understand them. While the painting everyone must understand. If only they would realize that an artist works above all of necessity."[7]

What the artist fears is not ambiguity but its denial. The arts can thrive only when ambiguity restricts the critics and the simplifiers, those who authoritatively demand clarity and denotation. Superficiality and distortion are the result of such Philistinism which denies both the freedom and the authenticity of the artist and the spectator. What the artist hopes for is that a creative engagement will take place between each spectator and the work of art. The meaning, as we have noted, is in the engagement, not solely in the work of art or the person. "We are not," writes John Cage, "in these dances and music, saying something. We are simple-minded enough to think that if we were saying something we would use words. We are rather doing something. The meaning of what we do is determined by each one who sees and hears it."[8]

The New Humanism has accepted and defends the ambiguity of limitation. In one sense humanism, even of the classical type, has always been aware of limitation and open to new insights about the nature of man and the nature of his context. But classical humanism measured and evaluated such insights in terms of its own *essential* definition, in terms of the good, the true, and the reasonable. The New Humanism, however, places the emphasis on existential expression rather than essential definition. Consequently, ambiguity plays a genuine role in its expression. Time and history, rather than the categories of abstract thought, become the contextual factors in meaningful human expression. For life lived here-and-now, the appropriate response must be here-and-now which eliminates any appeal to an absolute or suprahistorical standard. My response, that is my self-expression, must be in terms of my participation in *Being*, my historical perspective, and my anticipation of the contextual response to my own act.

Because any act of mine can be truly appropriate only once (though one must admit that variations on such common expressions as "thank you" surely can't vary much), any attempt to fix my character or judge my authenticity by a single act or series of acts, I highly resist. I am not bound to the pattern of past actions. What was appropriate *then* may be inappropriate *now*; what was authentic *then* becomes inauthentic *now*. It is true that people, both individually and corporately, tend to act in terms of behavioral patterns—there are communities which have voted Republican, and others Democratic, ever since the Civil War—but that is not so much a denial of the New Humanists' assertions as it is an illustration of what is meant by inauthenticity. A community which has constantly continued one party in power is not meritorious but moribund. A man who argues for "rugged individualism" in a technological age is not a champion of virtue but a child of ignorance.

What the New Humanism fears is that establishment of absolute "values" by which Western civilization has traditionally judged itself, its adequacy, and its progress. In any confrontation with such "values," where one is publicly forced to justify his position, the results are forced into categories of "good" or "evil," "yes" or "no," "black" or "white." For the New Humanism such absolute categories—suprapersonal, supratemporal—simply have no relevance. The validity of human action is not established in terms of the consistency of my interpretation of life but in terms of the consistency of my continuous reinterpretation of life. What counts is my responsiveness to the openness of others, to the affirmation of the world, to the time-full expression of *Being* in myself. Everything that is affects me and in part defines me. Even the rejection of what I believe to be the inauthentic is part of that continuous definition of self. No form of knowledge, scientific, artistic, *et al.*, is inappropriate to that task.

However, all this openness to life about us and this constant need for reinterpretation would seem to lead us into severe problems of relativism. Any system which lauds limitation, which adulates ambiguity, is asking for trouble. When everything is valid, when anything goes, then nothing is valid and nothing goes. Complete relativity results in complete anarchy, and complete anarchy is *meaningless*. That which saves the New Humanism from such meaninglessness is the expression of *Being* and/or the presence of God. While such expressions of *Being* or God do not provide an essence, an absolute, they do provide a guide. If judgment of appropriate action were totally random or chance, it would hardly be "appropriate" or, for that matter, meaningful. It is this problem which shall be discussed in the following chapter.

Another great problem for the New Humanist is that we live in a world dominated by technology. It is the precise, explicit, monolithic world of mathematics for which inaccurate, ambiguous, or ambivalent responses are the enemies. Nuances are nonsense to computer calculation. Consequently one can see the problems which result from such either/or existence in which clarity and definition are constantly demanded. In the Detroit, Michigan, riots in July, 1967, the Governor of the State needed Federal troops to provide protection for public and private property and to safeguard the lives of Detroit citizens. The Federal authorities asked that the Governor use the word "insurrection" so that the Government could not be accused of usurping State sovereignty. The Governor declined to use the word, for its use would void insurance coverage of the damage. Consequently, valuable time was lost because of a technicality. Such can be the tragic personal cost of living in an either/or world.

On the other hand, one can see the problems which result in a technological either/or world when clarity is ignored and definitions are left ambiguous. The Vietnam war is a flagrant example. Because the war began as a "police action" no limits were set, no position of policy clearly set forth. As a consequence there seem to be no limits to the escalation of hostilities. Almost by default we have become committed to war. It is possible to argue that the ambiguity which permits escalation also permits de-escalation. But the context has changed, and the ambiguity which permitted that escalation seems no longer to exist. New policies of prestige and national pride have altered the picture. The distribution and establishment of power do not permit a discrete withdrawal.

All-or-nothing situations are utterly antithetical to the New Humanism, but technology is here to stay. The question becomes that of how the two can coexist. This is *the* question of the New Morality which is the social expression of the New Humanism. However, it is first necessary to discuss the effect of ambiguity on both secular and sacred thought. The New Morality will be considered in the final chapter.

six: Ambiguity—secular and sacred

THE LAST CHAPTER, focusing on the ambiguity inherent in the New Humanism, raised the specter of relativism. While attempting to avoid the limiting structures of traditional metaphysics, ambiguity would seem to be in danger of courting chaos. Loss of meaning through the impersonality of philosophical categories can hardly seem much worse than loss of meaning through lack of relevance. Consequently, it is necessary to see what the New Humanism does in terms of the preservation of meaning.

What needs to be pointed out now has been hinted at before but never made explicit. While we have discussed the New Humanism thus far as though it was unitary, there are two expressions—one secular and one sacred. This does not mean that they treat the categories of authenticity, freedom, and affirmation in radically different ways. The basic agreement of the secular and religious humanisms, particularly in social expression, is one reason why the two forms have been equally sensitive to such current issues as integration, concern for peace, poverty programs, urbanization, automation, etc. Though the categories of these humanisms remain the same for each, the character of each differs because one is oriented toward *Being* and the other toward God. Therefore we must look at each of these orientations and see how each preserves meaning at such a fundamental level in terms of ambiguity.

For the New Humanism in its secular form, orientation in *Being* is the factor which prevents ambiguity from splintering existence into a meaningless relativism. Because the classical Greek tradition is so strong for most of us, such an orientation in *Being* would imply some form of monism—one final and absolute point of reference as the source for meaning. *Being*, we surmise, is the *one* Absolute which gives the *many* aspects of our life their identity. But this is just what the New Humanism does *not* claim. In its view, the problem of monism versus pluralism, of the one and the many, simply does not exist. In fact, the New Humanist insists that such a problem can only be formulated in terms of traditional Greek metaphysics. Monism is an abstract, nontemporal problem, not a problem of time-full *Being*, and therefore it is a spurious problem. If monism in any of its forms could somehow be established, it would define, clarify, and fix meaning in such a way that ambiguity would be eliminated—but then, so would "life."

Being is ambiguous simply because *Being* cannot be defined; it can only be lived, received, met, and encountered. As I consider my own *Being*, I recognize that while I am an agent in its continuance I am not responsible for its creation nor can I willfully continue or sustain it. I recieve it as a gift and remain continuously dependent on it. Therefore, I cannot do more than live it, for the only *Being* I truly know is *now* and the only certainty I have of my own *Being* is in the remembered past. But even this is too presumptuous a statement, for at any present moment I don't really "know" *Being*; I simply *am* it. If I can say in any way that I am objectively aware of *Being* now, I am most aware of it in the *Thous* which continuously engage me, i.e., I meet *Being* within the *I-Thou* relation when I am conscious of my *Thou*.

Thus *Being's* mode is ambiguous, for while I "am" it, I can never "know" it. The minute that I become *self*-conscious, *Being* eludes me. The self of which I am conscious is now a self out of the past. True *Being* remains with that observing self which is the only and real expression of *Being*. Self-transcendence is only possible because of the gift of time and memory. I can only "know" *Being* once-removed and therein is revealed the ambiguity in *Being*.

Being is ambiguous in still another way. *Being* is ambiguous because it involves me in the constant possibility of my *Non-being*. The possibility of death is the constant companion of the possibility of life, and I am unable to command either one. But *Non-being* is not only or primarily a threat to physical existence; it also threatens my existence-in-meaning. Since *Being* is time-full, i.e., now, so the expression of my *Being* is now. To be is to live authentically, that is, in the present. To live continuously in the past (for the unambiguous security of its fixity) or to live in the future (fixed by imagination) is not to live at all. Such attempts to escape are inauthentic and therefore participate in *Non-being*. This dual ambiguity of *Non-being* produces an anxiety, the threat of nothingness, which Heidegger believes results in a dual response: heroic self-assertion (which is shared by such existentialist thinkers as Jean-Paul Sartre and Albert Camus) and gratitude for *Being*. It would appear that the orientation for New Humanist meaning resides more in the second than in the first of these responses. Heroic self-assertion moves in terms of a defiance of *Nothing* which would seem to indicate a final relativism; all action is arbitrary and all values personal. On the other hand, gratitude for *Being* moves in terms of *Being* itself in an expression we have earlier called "affirmation." Because the New Humanism is more in keeping with this alternative, let us look at this orientation in *Being*.

Heidegger believes that *"Being*-in-time is its own ground," which would seem to deny any orientation just as effectively as Sartre's "defiance of Nothing," but this is not the total picture. Just because *Being* involves time, history must be understood as a dimension of *Being*. Our historical records are simply *Being's* objective expression. History may not be able to account for *Being*, or to encompass *Being*, but what it has done and continues to do is to reveal a consistency in *Being's* expression which provides us with as much insight into *Being* itself as the ambiguity of *Being*-in-time could permit. There is in history, for example, a consistency of rationality which has by continual development through the centuries produced what we have described as the technological world. What we have decried earlier is not the existence of this technological world, but its complete dominance in the lives of man. The world of computers is an incredibly secure, logical expression of one aspect of *Being*; so much so that we entrust our anxious lives to it everytime we travel by ship or plane. The ambiguity is evident not only in the fact that I never board a plane without first purchasing flight insurance, but also in the fact that I realize my life consists of more than mere travel.

This consistency in rationality is also evident in Heidegger's "unitary" theory of truth which was described earlier. That is, in history there is verification of a consistency in the expression of *Being* which actuates both myself and the world. The theory cannot validate itself, but experience can substantiate it. Yet, again, a degree of ambiguity exists, for I know that despite my correct and consistent judgments about the world, my life has also been plagued by incorrect and inconsistent judgments. How often we would like to "turn back the clock" or to "stop the world" so that we might get off. We become painfully aware of the limitation of our power of reason and of the scope of reason itself, while we are acknowledging our gratefulness and indebtedness to it.

There is more than simply the ambiguity of my own reason and its limitations; there is also in *Being* the ambiguity of truth itself which is not understood as an end, a goal, something finally to be achieved. Truth is understood as a revelation of *Being*. Because *Being* is time-full, it is also eventful, and eventfulness speaks for itself if we will let ourselves be sensitive to it. But such "revelation" is ambiguous, for it both presents and conceals itself, much like the smile of the "Mona Lisa," or the miniwink of an attractive *Thou*. Thus we are caught up by ambiguity which indicates but does not prescribe, which confirms but does not sanction, which judges but does not decree. Because such ambiguity exists, scholarship exists and will never end, science exists and will continue in research, and love exists and is never sated. Needless to say the ambiguity of my own response can result in the demise of any of these for me. All of these examples indicate that for the New Humanism truth is a relational complex which exists in time; it is not an abstract principle or absolute goal by which events are measured. *Being* provides orientation but not order, and ambiguity provides the possibility of meaning.

My *Being*-here-and-now is also given direction in terms of the act of encounter. What I "know" existentially and what is confirmed by past experience is that genuine meeting precipitates meaning—that encounter with the world, not withdrawal from it, produces a sense of well-being and happiness otherwise lost in isolation. The experience of "falling in love" is simply the most dramatic form of it. My life seems fullest when it is filled with my existence rather than with my introspection, my openness to the world rather than my withdrawal. Such encounter, as indicated earlier, is a creative act which, because it involves the world, finds life meaningful rather than absurd. Absurdity for the New Humanism is the product of isolation, inauthenticity, or faulty metaphysics—not life itself.

One of the immediate implications of this meaning-in-encounter is a social responsibility. Life is understood as a corporate venture—not because of a religious ideal, political ideal, historical ideal, or economic ideal—but simply because of its ontological nature. *Being* simply expresses itself most fully in a corporate way, and our response follows naturally enough. It is a well-known fact that much of the malaise of contemporary society is because of our isolation. The use of drugs, love-ins, and experimental neighborhoods are all efforts to establish a context within which a meaningful encounter can again take place. As opposed to the isolationism of Black Nationalism, Black Power, and White Citizens Councils, the great appeal of the civil rights movement to the American liberal—Black and White—has been the achievement of integration. Militant racial isolation runs contrary to all hope for a meaningful society.

The act of encounter, in which *Being* reveals itself, likewise gives orientation to my life-lived-here-and-now. My relationships with the *Its*, the things of this world, instruct me about who I am physically, about my place in the physical context, and about my role in social-political-economic structures of my society. My relationships with *Thous*, with other people with whom I experience an intricate personal relation, involve me in a depth of personal meaning characterized by a sense of fulfillment, identity, and affection. Each of these basic relationships provides guidance for an authentic existence.

Our lives are given orientation by yet one more aspect of *Being*, that aspect which we have termed earlier, "affirmation." It is true that *Being* carries with it the threat of *Non-being*, the anxiety of death—

In a thousand variations our religions, our poetry, our philosophies, our proverbial wisdom, bring home to us in this life from womb to grave, from war to war, the eschatological truth that "on us and all our race the slow, sure doom falls pitiless and dark"; that "all lovely things must have an ending, all lovely things must fade and die"; that "even this will pass away"; that "in the midst of life we are in death." . . .[1]

However, since death, and even *Non-being*, participate in the ambiguity which contours our *Being*, we are not completely discouraged or defeated by such a threat. We may perceive on the edges of *Being* the shadows of *Non-being*, but as time-full *Beings* we are even more immediately and powerfully aware of our ability to create, to withstand adversity, to evaluate, to control, to reason. The act of *Being*, which is now, is affirmative. One is paralyzed by *Non-being* and death only when one has given up life. When the future, the anticipation of death, looms larger than the present, then life has become inauthentic.

Within the context of my ambiguous relationship to *Being*, orientation and meaning exist: the consistency of my rational life, the revelation of history, the fulfillment of encounter, and the affirmation of power (all of which exhibit ambiguity) grant to the new secular humanist direction and intentionality. The "final or ultimate questions" concerning life are simply not asked, because for the New Humanist they do not exist; the final judgment does not take place because there is no final judge and no final standard. Rather —customs, rules, and laws come and go, formulated by our reason, in accordance with our understanding of corporate responsibility, schooled by our interpretation of history—all in terms of a life-lived-here-and-now.

Having considered the orientation for life in terms of *Being* and ambiguity, it is time to turn our attention to those New Humanists who find their orientation for meaning in terms of God and ambiguity. Perhaps the first thing which should be noted is that such an orientation is not fundamentally motivated by a rejection of secularist humanism. It is true that representatives of the new religious humanism concur with Buber's judgment that Heidegger's understanding of *Being* represents a "closed system," but the secular humanists have at least modified their stance because of Buber's criticisms. It is also true that the religious humanist believes the secular expression of humanism is incapable of adequately treating the character and force of evil—the conscious and willful destruction of authentic life. Evil as the betrayal of one self in *Being* does not carry the power of the betrayal of a relationship to God characterized by love. This criticism, however, is a relative one, for evil receives its direction and power from the affirmative ground it denies.

The orientation of religious humanism in God is not simply an identity of God with *Being*-itself, attractive as that might at first appear to be. Heidegger, in his "Letter on Humanism" suggests that such a connection might exist. The truth of *Being* which is revealed to man and to which one responds Heidegger calls "the holy," and it is from the essense of this holiness that the essence of deity is conceived. It is only in this context that one is aware of that for which the name "God" is appropriate. But such an argument does not motivate the religious humanist. The objection which he has to this argument is not, as some scholars have suggested, that it appeals to immanentism and consequently results in an anthropology rather than a theology; his objection is that secular humanism is simply inadequate to describe the experience of reality as the religious humanist lives it, i.e., encounters it. In short the religious humanist appeals to an awareness of God in and through the *I-Thou* encounter. Within this context God reveals Himself. Of course this at once raises all the problems of private and public knowledge. The only possible way of overcoming these problems is to claim that what the secularist experiences in the *I-Thou* encounter and what the man of faith experiences in that encounter are one and the same. The problem with this solution is at least twofold. The secularist will see no need to add "God" to a situation which is explicable in simpler, more "natural" ways; the religionist will say that he has been where the secularist is now and that the experience of faith is qualitatively different. As a result, the New Humanism within faith simply accepts the burden of a private knowledge which it acknowledges to be ambiguous.

The man of faith claims that in the time-fullness of the present he is constantly being addressed by God who stands over and against him as his *Thou*. It is the *Eminent-Thou* who meets him and gives his life its meaning and its identity within the context of encounter.

Before exploring this claim of man's orientation in God, it should be noted that this New Theology carries with it the same time-full ontology that the secular orientation exhibits. Translated into religious terms, the primary affirmation is: God *is*. In affirming this, the New Theology avoids the metaphysical problem which has plagued religious thinkers ever since the early Church Fathers tried to synthesize Greek metaphysical monism with Hebraic religious monotheism: the problem of divine transcendence.

Although this problem has been briefly mentioned before, it should be explored further simply because there is so much misunderstanding about the issues involved, both outside and inside the context of faith. Simply stated, if God is transcendent—above and beyond all worlds—can man possibly have any contact, any awareness of Him? If God is immanent—within creation, within man—then do we not have merely an anthropology rather than theology? Can God be both at once—transcendent and immanent? That, strictly speaking, is a contradiction in terms, which is nonsense; and nonsense is not at all what faith has claimed to be. To submit one's thought to the discipline of a logic only to deny its validity at the crucial point, is to vitiate the power of the total position.

Within Western tradition, transcendence has implied that God is perfect, eternal, and immutable and that the world is becoming, time-full, and changing. These notions, in terms of a meaningful encounter between God and man, are simply incompatible, and, if we follow through with their implications, not at all what faith has wanted. It means, for instance, that if God is already perfect, then His creation is ultimately insignificant, inferior, in fact meaningless to Him. Such divine immutability means that there can be no *genuine* encounter with God, for a genuine encounter affects both participants. If God cannot be affected, then relationship to Him would be similar to a relationship to a principle or a law, which certainly is not what faith has claimed. Such an immutable God would also deny the validity of prayer— for prayer is a response, a thanksgiving, a petition, a confession—and what are these to an immutable Being? Love which characterizes the *I-Thou* encounter demands mutuality and response. If the objection is raised at this point that traditional Western religious thought has always included love, along with immutability, as one of the primary characteristics of God, it must be replied that this portion of tradition is not Greek but Hebraic; and even though history has juxtaposed these characteristics, we clearly cannot logically hold them together. Such logical contradictions (and others like them) are the stuff out of which contemporary agnostics are made.

Under such confused metaphysical conditions as these, to give glory to God is to take it away from man, and to give glory to man is to take it away from God. It was precisely this issue of God's transcendence versus His immanence which recently precipitated the theologically sharp, personally sad, controversy between the two Swiss theologians, Karl Barth and Emil Brunner. Brunner believed that God's goodness and glory were meaningless to man if there were no "point of contact" within the human being through which such characteristics could be perceived and understood. Barth rejected this as an old argument of natural theology by which man could achieve his own salvation, or could "demonstrate" God, or could argue to His existence. Although Barth has perhaps softened his argument by speaking now of the "Humanity of God," this has in fact not solved the basic problem but has simply made it more complex.

The New Humanism as an expression of religious faith rejects the whole transcendent-immanent problem as a representation of Western metaphysics, not faith itself. The New Humanism begins within the new ontology of God's *Being*, which speaks of the reality of God as time-full, not timeless. It is for this reason that one replaces the phrase *"Eminent Thou"* for Buber's phrase *"Eternal Thou."* The change in phrase is representative of the change in orientation—from the cosmological (eternal) to the ontological (eminent-now).

To make such a change is to move from the Absolute to the ambiguous, from God the Infinite to God the Father. The New Humanist orientation in God is within the *I-Thou* encounter. In such an encounter I know who I am in relation to Him who engages me so completely, fundamentally, and deeply that I call Him "Father." I use "Father" as a historical symbol which is significant to the community of faith and is faithful to the nature of the confrontation. But the whole encounter with God is very ambiguous. I know and I do not know; I believe and I doubt; I love and I hate; I am loved and I am estranged; and I am sustained but I do not know why or how. The limitation of my *Being* marks the limitation of my understanding. Consequently, I respond in "faith" (trust) as I respond to those human beings whom I love and who love me, for I know that even with them the relationship is ambiguous—one of knowing and not knowing, yet trusting. Though such a relationship to God is never absolute, I find it to be most meaningful to me. This encounter, unlike scientific facts, or critical history, or aesthetics informs me in a most intimate way "who I am." Therefore my response is critical, sensitive, personal, and dramatic—in a word, existential. It is only under these circumstances that one can truly understand the Old Testament response to the presence of God as one of love, yet also of awesomeness: the *mysterium tremendum*. The encounter is time-full and meaningful in context; it is not a principle or a law one meets, but *Him*.

The ambiguity, of course, is evident in the limitation of the encounter. I cannot know God, i.e., comprehend Him, I can only respond to Him—just as I cannot fully comprehend someone I love, but only respond with varying degrees of trust.

What, then, can be said about the many sources of authority which have traditionally been associated with religion, particularly Christianity? Here the ambiguity works both ways by denying absolutism but permitting historical continuity. If my knowledge of God really turns out to be an awareness of God now, then, for confirmation, I must turn to history and tradition (my own and other's), just as secular humanism does for its orientation to *Being*.

One of the most evident sources of authority for Judaism and Christianity has been the Scriptures. These are the writings of men of faith, to which subsequent generations have turned for inspiration and guidance. For a time these writings were considered the literal words of God Himself—which did, of course, give them an authority verging on the absolute. But theological and Biblical scholarship has clearly excluded the possibility of such bibliolatry. However, such scholarship has also established that there are at least three things distinctive about these "sacred" writings. First, they cover crucial moments in the histories of the Jewish and Christian peoples—the Exodus from Egypt, the rise and fall of the monarchies, the Exile, the Restoration, the life of Jesus, and the establishment of the Church. Second, they speak directly and "mythologically" of the nature and experience of man's encounter with God. Third, they have recorded these events and these encounters with such graphic fidelity and accuracy that generations of men have been able to identify with them, to find an articulation for their own loving and despairing relationships to God.

The ambiguity of such authority is immediately evident, for subjective confirmation is never absolute proof. It is likewise true that the witness of Scripture alone is not authoritative enough to convince the skeptic. To read the Gospel of Mark ten times does not necessarily convince the reader of the reality of Jesus' messianic role, even though it may assure him that this is the man about whom the Church so speaks. Such ambiguity assures the skeptic his spiritual freedom and personal integrity at the same time that it confirms the faith of the man who believes.

For others in the Judeo-Christian tradition, authority rests with mystical revelation even more than with Scripture, though such revelation is often mediated by Scripture. But whether one thinks of revelation as the transmission of facts or information, or less denotatively as the experience of God's presence which one must interpret himself, the ambiguity of any such subjective or private experience is immediately evident. We are too sophisticated now to accept as absolute and irrefutable even the most powerful of spiritual experiences. Needless to say, the consistency of such experiences, their similarity to the experiences of other men of faith, their correlation with the witness of Scripture, and their affirmation of life tend to reassure us of their validity. However, response to such revelation is not unlike the experience of "falling in love"—it is a private knowledge, powerful, convincing, but always ambiguous. For the validity of both experiences, we use the term "self-authenticating"—yet there are times when both have turned out to be inauthentic interpretations or psychological projections. Revelation is likewise subject to another expression of ambiguity because it occurs within the *I-Thou* encounter, i.e., now. What is revealed to me now, in this context, will not be the same in another context, in another moment in time. This continually new revelation becomes the active denial of immutable principles and absolutes that would in effect silence the Word of God.

The Church itself has also served as a source of final authority, particularly in the Roman Catholic tradition. The Church, instituted by the Christ, considered to be the "body" with the Christ its "head," considered by others to be the "bride" of the Christ, stands as the point of mediation between the world and God. However, the new religious humanism does not see the Church in such a supratemporal or authoritative position. In part this is because of the ambiguity of Scripture and mystical revelation which we have already examined. If these are not ultimate authorities, then no institution which establishes its own authority on the basis of their claims can be considered ultimately authoritative. No such finality can be attributed to any temporal revelation which appeals to the metaphysical authority of truth—e.g., such as has been claimed for papal infallibility. "Infallibility" is too strong a word for the ambiguity of the historical and spiritual context of Christianity to support. The Church, whether it be directly attributable to the person of Jesus or not, represents those people of like mind, dedication, and faith, who have been called together so that they might realize among themselves an extent and kind of authenticity they believe normative—even though unrealized—for all mankind. The Church is an acknowledgment of the centrality of the "Person" of God for our temporal life, a recognition of our historical lineage and indebtedness, an acknowledgment of the corporate nature of all humanity, a celebration of the joy of living, and an affirmation of life as encounter-in-love. Its relevance is possible because of its responsive ambiguity, its ability to function in a continuously changing context. The tragedy of the contemporary Church is that it is *not* contemporary. Though some exciting experimentation is taking place, it is not central to the institution of the Church; it is the patronized escape valve for so-called radicals. The Protestant Church is still in the nineteenth century with its Church School and Sermon; the Roman Church antedates this. But strikingly enough, through the decisions and spirit of Vatican II, Roman Catholicism may reach the twentieth century before Protestantism. If the Church is to be the institutional power representing the "people of God" in the institutionalized, technocentric twentieth century, then it must recall its sense of ambiguity, its need to be *now* in a changing world.

The ambiguity of reason has been previously discussed, but it, too, has traditionally been a source of absolute authority in religious life, e.g., reason considered to be man's *"Imago Dei"* so that reason must be the common characteristic, the point of contact, between God and man. The ambiguity which we now know characterizes reason cannot long support such a contention. Even though reason's contribution is paramount to most human endeavor, it, too, has its limitations in time, kind, and scope.

The one authority central to all of Christianity is the person of Jesus. No matter what claims are made about this man—that He is God, or God's Son, or a subordinate to God, or God's elected Son, or a very good man sensitive to God's will—he is central and authoritative for Christian history, thought, and action. Yet even here ambiguity plays a decisive role. The very fact that within the tradition itself such varied interpretations of the person of Jesus can be so devoutly championed is indicative of the limitation of Scripture, revelation, reason, and the Church. Yet here, again, we must remind ourselves that such ambiguity does not imply an absolute relativity, and no one has stated this more clearly than H. Richard Niebuhr. The variety of portraits of Jesus in Christian thought

. . . cannot obscure the fundamental unity which is supplied by the fact that the Jesus Christ to whom men are related in such different ways is a definite character and person whose teachings, actions, and sufferings are of one piece. . . . Important as are the once debated questions whether Jesus ever "really" lived, and the still moot problem of the trustworthiness of New Testament records as factual descriptions of actual events, these are not the questions of primary significance. For the Jesus Christ of the New Testament is in our actual history, in history as we remember and live it, as it shapes our present faith and action. And this Jesus Christ is a definite person, one and the same whether he appears as man of flesh and blood or as risen Lord. He can never be confused with a Socrates, a Plato, or an Aristotle, a Gautama, a Confucius, or a Mohammed, or even with an Amos or Isaiah. . . . However great the variations among Christians in experiencing and describing the authority Jesus Christ has over them, they have this in common: that Jesus Christ is their authority, and that the one who exercises these various kinds of authority is the same Christ.[2]

The New Humanist would term the authority of which Niebuhr speaks in this passage as authority voluntarily accepted. The centrality of Christ in one's life is a decision based upon the sense of divine presence in the I-Thou encounter, the historical and cultural heritage within which one interprets and understands such an encounter, the correlation, even sense of identity, between that encounter and that heritage, and the exemplification in the life of Jesus of those attributes of Being which we have called the New Humanism—authenticity, freedom, and affirmation. He was one who was open to all men, who considered life ultimately more precious than law, and who affirmed the meaningfulness of all creation.

For the New Humanist whose orientation is in his encounter with God, meaning is given in terms of that encounter and the tradition which provides the context for it. Both are ambiguous, both limited, so that decisions for action and thought can never be absolute or definitively righteous. The New Humanist whose orientation is God, recognizes that there is no such thing as a Jewish God, or a Christian God, or an Islamic Allah, although there are these various traditions for expressing the meaning and Being of God. Through them one is the recipient of the great and varied richness of the past: its wisdom, its judgment, and its continuity with the present. Such traditions become treacherous only when some relative expression, e.g., a way of prayer, an organization of the congregation, a specific relationship to society in general, becomes absolutized, fixed, and sanctified. Such absolutizing of religious tradition is the most dangerous form of idolatry because it breeds a concomitant self-right-eousness, destroys the present, and substitutes an *It* for the *Thou* of God. The basic question for the life oriented in God is not the historical question nor the technological question, but the question of meaning for the life of faith lived here-and-now.

seven: Towards the new morality

BECAUSE THE HUMANIST revolution in thought, expression, and act has been so widespread, the effects are everywhere noticeable. One cannot be exposed daily to our new art forms, new literary forms, new musical expressions, and new theologies and philosophies without being profoundly concerned about and affected by the radical changes they present and symbolize. Though one may reject many of these changes as immature, incomprehensible, irrational, or just plain phony, they have made an impressive impact on our society and, for that matter, on the world. Our electronics revolution—radio, films, television, computers—has only served to intensify and accelerate this impact by making possible and accessible an audio-visual exposure to these radical changes. We are, according to Marshall McLuhan, tribalizing the world.

The theologian Paul Tillich puts the end of the nineteenth century at World War I, but this event is not just the end of that century. It is, Tillich rightly claims, the end of one era and the beginning of another. Surely the course of our study thus far substantiates such a judgment. The whole fabric of our culture is being worked over by some very visible weavers, and it is difficult to establish at this point whether they are merely patching or actually re-weaving a whole new cloth. Consequently, what has been celebrated recently under the simplistic banner of "The New Morality" tends to be a representative mixture of destruction and reformation.

With the ending of an era comes the collapse of old standards, old values, old norms—in short, the old morality. In our own situation, when Absolutes are called into question, when Form itself is questioned, the result is an accelerated deterioration of traditional moral standards which have been variously labeled "the Victorian ethic," "the Protestant ethic," "middle class values," "the American way," and so on. Stability, particularly in terms of predictability, has disappeared. We no longer know what is "right" for us to do as individuals or as a nation. For example, the ethical principles and simple, straight-forward injunctions once thought central and adequate for the national ideal—liberty, justice, equality, freedom of press, freedom of speech, freedom of opportunity —have crumbled under the pressures of the complexities of twentieth-century life. One can no longer realistically expect that all emergent nations will have the American form of democracy any more than one can realistically respond to a Wilsonian plea to "make the world safe for democracy." What we now know is that no one nation can totally and effectively control its own destiny let alone the destiny of the world. *Pax Americana* may be a glorious wish, but it is certainly not a realistic picture of the political realities of the late twentieth century.

Since discovering that we as Americans have not cornered or monopolized the truth market and have had to compete with other viable political and economic systems, our self-righteousness and our assurance have been shaken. Our national posture has gradually sagged into an expediency relative to self-interest, as the struggle in South-East Asia indicates. The traditional words, though still used, are all too often not attempts at redefinition but, rather, totem terms invoked by confused or frightened citizens in the desperate hope that sheer repetition of the words themselves will somehow reestablish the power of the principle; or such words are often calculated cliches in the mouths of some "superpatriots," politicians and laymen alike, who want to justify injustice and their own self-interests. The growing "credibility gap" (as a two-way gap) between the government and the people is the result. Such civil sickness can only increase, with dissident groups of all kinds becoming increasingly self-seeking and militant, if the loss of national integrity continues. The growing polarities in America over the issues of race and war are evidence of such a trend.

Other examples of the moral confusion of this transition period are not hard to find. We no longer know what is "right" for us to do about the relations among labor, management, and government. The interests of all three are so interlocking that any deviation can cause a national crisis. The old rules about hard work and honest bargaining just do not apply: one cannot bargain with the boss or "catch his eye" when one's point of contact is a management time study or a union quota system; individual unions and industries must abandon much local bargaining for "industry-wide" sessions; labor and management together must now face a government which not only controls and limits their activities to a degree but, in some cases, even becomes a competitor; the government can no longer simply concern itself with domestic issues, for foreign markets and common markets make economics a world problem. So the economic problem and its accompanying moral dilemmas become acute. The coal miner in West Virginia feels the impact of the world, but his credit is still calculated by the local grocery store.

We no longer know what is "right" to do about the problems of interpersonal relations, particularly in the area of sex. Education, population problems, the "pill," and loss of the sacramental nature of marriage all have eaten away at the traditional cultural patterns. Taboos once observed for no other reason than that they were "right and proper" for generations cannot persuade or convince the contemporary questioning mind. Extravagant theological threats ("God will make you impotent!") no longer strike fear into hearts of teenagers or anyone else. Social ostracism for, or legal restraint of, so-called "deviant behavior" is no longer an unavoidable threat. The fear of pregnancy has been removed from sexual intercourse so that this physical expression of "love" has been freed from the moral restraints of responsible paternity or maternity. The questions then are posed: "Why not love with the body as completely as with the heart?" and "Must such physical love necessarily be confined to marriage?" In an age of transition when new values are being established, the emotional, physical, and spiritual strains of the existing value void are often tragically evident in broken hearts, broken homes, and broken lives. Loss of authority has left a legacy of anxiety. The search for the New Morality is the search for new directions, not the repudiation of direction.

The citation of these three areas of acute moral concern as examples is enough to suggest the complexity of the problem. Old patterns are either inadequate or discarded, and, without new expressions, genuine confusion ensues. Some people courageously cling to the old values, the proverbial "good old days," terrified at what might happen if they abandoned them. Others courageously search for new patterns, new values which would provide a meaningful life, frightened that their experimentation may bring irremedial tragedy rather than fulfillment. Still others simply exploit the confusion to gratify their own self-interests, confident that there are no values other than one's own.

When one hears the term "New Morality," one is apt to find reference to any one of the above three possibilities, but particularly the latter two. The very last alternative, however, is representative of the ethics of nihilism and offers little that is constructive for us to consider. It is certainly not an expression of what we have termed the New Humanism.

The "New Morality" has been a catch-all phrase for all activity deviating from pre-World-War-I ethical norms. Yet it should be clearly understood that the breakdown of traditional standards we are witnessing about us, the seemingly inevitable disenchantment and frustration which results when the basis for a once-meaningful life has been threatened, is really only the prelude to the New Morality. But if there is to be a genuine New Morality, it will have to emerge not from the least common denominator of such moral decadence, but rather from some understanding of the implication, the contours, the nature of the New Humanism. Chaos alone can never be the matrix for spontaneous generation. Passive acceptance of the destructive forces at work in society is not the rôle of the New Humanist. What is urgently needed is the thoughtful creation of new and significant value structures. Until this affirmative response is made, the moral dilemma in which we find ourselves can only be intensified.

Before going further, terminology ought to be clarified. Normally the word "morality" is used to describe the value designation inherent or assumed in any specific human act or generally accepted custom. By contrast, the word "ethics" usually denotes a rational system of values which is both prescriptive and adjudicative. Thus to call an act "immoral" or "unethical" is really to misuse both terms. What we mean when we misuse such terms is quite clear: it is *not* that the act has no value at all; it is rather that the act is wrong or harmful either according to custom (morality) or according to system (ethics). Much of the confused talk about the New Morality reveals such a misunderstanding of these basic terms. What most people mean by the search for the New Morality is the search for a New Ethic. However, I have retained the term New Morality not only because of its popular acceptance but, more importantly, for the fact that we are discussing not so much an ethic as an ethos, a context, within which several ethical systems may coexist.

If the New Humanism, in both its secular and religious forms, is to give rise to a New Morality, then it should be possible to determine, on the basis of our study, some of the directions or contours of that morality. Taking as normative the ambiguity we have observed governing all human existence, capacities, and relationships, the New Morality should expect no exemption from such a limitation.

Our understanding of *Being* in terms of self-awareness is limited and elusive; our knowledge of God through the *I-Thou* encounter is private and hidden; our relationship to others is limited by the degree of our authenticity as well as theirs; our information about the physical world is provisional as well as being an apparent one-way rational appropriation; and all of these relationships are further limited by the time-fullness of *Being* in which we all participate here-and-now.

Under these circumstances, any New Morality must reflect such limitations in its rejection of absolute prescriptive ends—*the* Good, *the* Right, *the* Truth, *the* Kingdom—as well as absolute prescriptive laws—"obey the government without question," "obey the Bible without question," "obey the parent without question." Any expression of these goals or laws as absolutely inviolable would not only falsely deny the reality of ambiguity but would also establish a priority of abstract principle or law over self, an error Western tradition has made all too often. In the New Humanist's understanding of integrity, there are times when my integrity, or truth of *Being,* is contrary to, or cannot be limited to, the world of objectively verifiable facts, *i.e.,* I do not always tell the medical patient of his condition, or my hostess of her indigestible meal.

But having acknowledged this, one must immediately affirm that life can be *reasonably* lived only if goals or ends or standards such as "the good," "the right," "the truth," "the kingdom," are provisionally accepted; and that chaos can be averted in an inescapably social world only if one does, for example, intelligently obey the government and/or does imaginatively follow the ethical insights of Scripture.

The difference, of course, is immediately evident, for under these latter conditions such goals and such laws become *authoritative for our lives' but do not function as Absolutes.* Times, insights, and contexts change and, therefore, so must laws, means, and ends. I must so live in the condition of freedom that my authenticity as a self may be maintained even at the risk of defying the existing external authorities. This is not to plead for anarchy but for the constant reevaluation and restatement of that penultimate authority which would permit a continuous authentic expression of self and society. Such is my responsibility to the continuing demands of ambiguity.

The instances of civil disobedience in the American civil rights struggle are a case in point. As opposed to the anarchy and lawlessness of the ghetto riots, civil disobedience challenges the authority and effective justice of the existing laws by the deliberate violation of such laws and the self-surrender of the violators to the government. Such action brings the inadequacy of the laws or customs in question to the attention of society, and a fitting reform can be made. However, when such reforms prove empty or resulting legislation is powerless to enforce the reform, then more serious disobedience, even violence, can result—as we see in the urban riots. Human desperation does not recognize the authority of abstract Absolutes; pleas for sanity at such times appear to the desperate only as rejection, a banishment to futility and meaningless existence.

It is not at all amiss to note here that democracy as a form of government is structured on the reality of ambiguity as a human condition. The three-branch structure of the U.S. Government serves to preserve and honor that ambiguity so that an absolute rule can never be established while responsible authority is always maintained. This recognition of human limitation is reflected in Reinhold Niebuhr's celebrated dictum from *The Children of Light and the Children of Darkness*: "Man's capacity for justice makes democracy possible; but man's inclination to injustice makes democracy necessary."[1] Ambiguity as a human condition of *Being* must be reflected in the condition of social and political organization.

The use of the descriptive term "penultimate" is questionable, a case of ambiguity in point. "Penultimate" conveys the idea of next-to-final in principle, power, or purpose and implies that there is an ultimate which *is*, even though such an ultimate is unknown or unknowable, not yet attained or attainable. But this is not what the New Humanist wants to convey by such a word, for such usage brings metaphysical absolutism in by the semantic back door. "Penultimate" authority should suggest for us the natural, reasonable, authentic expression of *Being*—more specifically of my *Being* and the correlated objective world of "Things" which reveal themselves to me and are related to me in terms of *Being Itself*. Thus my relationship to fire or water carries its own natural authority or expression which I violate at my own peril. In other words, the "penultimate" authority, those rules and laws by which I partially govern my existence, is simply the natural expression of the *I-It* world about which Martin Buber writes. Such rules and laws are discerned through experience, by experimentation, not through Platonic metaphysical speculation.

The issue becomes more complicated when one adds to the *I-It* relation the relational world of *Thou*. Three things are immediately discernible. First, authority is established, as in the relation to *Its,* by experience; that is, the relationship establishes its own authenticity and is thereby self-governed. Second, the authority of the *I-Thou* relationship takes priority over the *I-It* relationship, a priority not only of origin but also in *Being*. This priority, for example, is the implicit justification behind the appealing lyrics of "I can't give you anything but love. . . ." And third, the world of potential *Thous* forms and constitutes a particular world of *Its* (businesses, organizations, communities we call society, and this world —as in the other relational situations—forms its own laws, principles, goals, and relational structures, natural to the *I-It* context. As before, experience, which we call history, informs us of the general nature of that relationship, and does so with enough accuracy that we speak of it (and of such related disciplines as economics and sociology) as social science.

The problem is further complicated by the fact that any of these *I-It* relationships with other people who constitute society, can at any moment become an *I-Thou* relationship, and when this occurs, the priorities which govern my decision-making undergo significant change. As an American businessman I know that only law, order, and stability can provide the climate for commercial growth and prosperity, but as a man with intimate friends within some American minority group, I may choose to defy the "City Council" and march in the streets to secure equality for my friends, to the detriment of my own business. Though I have a profound respect for equality and justice, what really sends me into the streets is not the thought of future financial benefits but the love of my friend.

As priorities change, so do my actions and so do those of all men. Thus the picture of human society is continuously being refocused. All men need to act in such a way that personal and public responsibilities, personal and public actions do not countermand each other. To ignore public responsibility (the world of *It*) is to end with anarchy; to ignore personal responsibility (the world of *Thou*) is to end with dehumanizing conformity. The answer is not merely compromise, for compromise implies that there is some unifying identity between the nature of the *It* world and the nature of the *Thou* world. But this is simply not the case. The "laws, principles, and ends" peculiar to society and the physical world are not those "laws, principles, and ends" peculiar to my personal life. The former we characterized by impersonally ordered relations, the latter by freedom, spontaneity, and decision.

This is part of the ambiguity of human existence. The limitation I experience in comprehension and action, "in *Being*," means that my life must be lived not in compromise, which itself hints at finality, but in tension and risk. Both *Thou* and *It* loyalties make their claims upon me; more important, both relationships help "define" me. To honor one may be to dishonor the other. But this is the risk which a time-full, ambiguous life runs. In the act of decision, I can use the word "compromise" only if by that word I imply a genuine consideration of the tensions upon me—not their resolution. My decision is made in tension and is carried out (for better or for worse) as a decision-intension. The security of finality is a luxury which ambiguity cannot afford and a snare which authenticity must avoid.

If ambiguity, as evidence in the New Humanism, is

normative for the New Morality, then it follows that some form of contextual ethic will emerge. The very fact that such divergent contemporary thinkers as Joseph Fletcher, Karl Barth, Joseph Sitler, Paul Lehmann, and H. Richard Niebuhr all propose some form of contextual ethic is reason enough to take seriously such a contention.

The "contextual ethic" obviously receives its name from the fact that ethical decisions are determined by assessing the context, the various forces—social, political, physical, economic, intellectual, spiritual—past, present, and future, which impose themselves upon us in our deliberations prior to or during any "value" decision. But to describe such an ethic is not to justify its use. A contextual ethic suggests itself as one natural expression for the New Humanism because it does take the ambiguity of existence into account; because it is totally inclusive of all those factors, deliberative and active, which constitute *Being*-in-the-world-here-and-now whether such *Being* is secular or religious; and because we note that the very process of decision-making involves all these factors —attention to our total self within its total orientation of meaning.

It follows, then, that although we acknowledge our dependence upon historical guidance, precedent, and wisdom no one standard or set of standards can be final for a contextual ethic which tries to take into account all the limiting factors involved in any given new context. In each decision one must ask, "What am I trying to achieve?" "What is known?" "What are the limits?" "What are the priorities?" "What will be the response to my decision?" "What act will, in fact, give the fullest expression to *Being*?" In any given situation, therefore, what we expect from one man we might not expect from another who is politically more powerful, or another better educated, or yet another who is mentally retarded. Likewise, the patterns of response and reward for the twentieth-century American are likely to be quite different from those of a contemporary man of a less advanced culture, though variations within any given culture complex are apt to be limited because of the focus of common forces.

A problem, of course, arises when the contextual ethic provides the opportunity for willful, selfish action. For both secularist and religionist such action, as noted in Chapter 5, is apostasy. For the secularist, it is the forsaking of the authentic expression of *Being,* the penalty for which is a self-inflicted isolation and loss of meaning. For the religionist, apostasy is the forsaking of God, the Eminent *Thou,* which carries a comparable penalty. For the secularist, restitution of authenticity within the *I-It* relationship is a matter of new insight which informs him of the ignorance and destructiveness of previous acts. For secularist and religionist alike, forgiveness alone can provide the possibility of a resumption and and renewal of the *I-Thou* relationship. Restitution involved in the *I-Thou* apostasy is more difficult to achieve than in the *I-It,* of course, for it involves the necessity both of forgiveness (renewed acceptance and trust) and of repentence (acknowledgement of betrayal and regret).

For some Cassandras the loss of absolute standards, principles, and goals can result only in destructive forces being indiscriminately released against an idyllic heritage. Yet "The backward look behind the assurance/Of recorded history, the backward half-look/Over the shoulder" does not, as Mr. T. S. Eliot reminds us in "The Dry Salvages," convince most of us of the unqualified sanctity of the past. The inhumanity of human behavior seems to be the expression more of allegiance to nonhuman Absolutes than of authentic response to the nature of *Being*—as God or man. Certainly the last fifty years of war, suffering, and growing disenchantment with Absolute demands have served to strengthen this conviction. This is not to resurrect the "noble savage" of Rousseau. It *is* to bring into question the assumption in Western thought that morality and ethics can be meaningfully expressed only with the context of, and as reflections of, an Absolute. One of the things which contemporary interest in the New Humanism seems to be displaying is a growing belief that metaphysical Absolutes such as *the* Good, *the* Truth, *the* Beautiful have really hampered man's free and open expression of *Being*—whether that be in art, music, literature, or morality—and that health can only be achieved when the *I-Thou* and *I-It* can time-fully express themselves. We cannot avoid the ambiguities of human existence, and we are tragically mislead if we believe that some ethical system can resolve them for us. Our present "sickness unto death" certainly is no witness for those who deprecate this contemporary revolution in the name of past holiness or of moral perfectionism.

For the contextual ethic, the ambiguities involved are both its strength and limitation. One of the finest of the contextualists, H. R. Niebuhr, brings this sharply into focus: decisions "are made, it appears, on the basis of relative insight and faith, but they are not relativistic. They are individual decisions, but not individualistic. They are made in freedom, but not in independence; they are made in the moment, but are not nonhistorical."[2] Each of these qualifications deserves further explication.

Niebuhr indicates that the decisions which we reach are relative in four ways: First, they are relative to our limited fragmentary knowledge—as anyone who has contemplated marriage, tried to discipline children effectively, or endeavored constructively to criticize government policy on international affairs surely knows. Second, decisions are relative to the extent of our belief and unbelief—as anyone recognizes who has hedged his commitments to God or man with mental reservations, hidden alternatives, or flight insurance. Third, decisions are relative to our historical and social context—as any first-generation American, any Vista or Peace Corps volunteer, or any Depression-age father and his hippie-age child dazedly admit. Finally, decisions are made relative to the values of our time—as most Victorians admit, gazing wonderingly at the guiltless sexual freedom of the present generation. Niebuhr makes these qualifications about our relative decisions within the Christian heritage, but as already indicated, such qualifications could equally well apply to secular humanism, though "belief" in such a case would be understood in terms of the affirmation of *Being* rather than faith in God.

The reasons that such decisions are relative and not relativistic are that they each find points of orientation, i.e., *Being* or God, from which all else is understood. But what is found is not an ultimate point of orientation nor is it a point of ultimate orientation. As we have noted earlier, both of these considerations, i.e., my understanding and my appropriation of Absolute Truth, are finally ambiguous. Decisions are only possible under such conditions; otherwise action would be a matter of resignation to either fate or chance. What we have found is a context which offers its own coherence within which my authenticity may be expressed. Thus as a Jew or a Christian, my authenticity is bound up with justice, mercy, and humility—all expressive of my belief, hedged as it is, by my unbelief or doubt. I do not make the claim that all life must be Judeo-Christian, but I do make the claim that my understanding of life is Judeo-Christian. Such an affirmation on my part does not necessitate a denial of the meaningfulness of all other contexts, Buddhist, for example, but it does demand that we search for some common ground for genuine encounter. If our contention about *Being* is correct, then its revelation must be evident in all contextual encounters.

The reason my decisions are individual but not individualistic is that my individuality is the result of my involvement, the *I-Thou* encounter. I can only know myself in terms of my social context, therefore I can act only out of that context. While I am responsible for my deliberate act, I am not equally responsible for my cultural context. If I display signs of prejudice, it is in part a response to existing elements in my society by which I have been conditioned. Anyone who has tried to overcome a sectional or racial prejudice knows with what difficulty and with how many relapses such a victory is won. If I am an advocate for new sexual mores, or for a radically New Humanism, these must be defined and and explained in terms of traditional expression, even if that amounts to a disavowal of that older tradition. Anyone who recognizes the statement, "I know the words you're using but I can't understand what you're saying" is aware of the problem. The individualistic decision simply does not exist; the reality of the here-and-now in which I live involves me with my contemporaries and links me to the past and to the future. But the confusion persists because the linkage is ambiguous; it is not simply the expression of some efficient cause.

My decisions are made in freedom but not in independence because of similar ambiguities. The reason that I use to come to a decision is not only fragmented and partial, it is also schooled by my society, my historical position, and my cultural stance. The time-full limitation of my existence brings my known, historical life continuously into contact with the unknown and the not-yet, so that I am continually impelled to be that which is new, even if it be only a new interpretation of the old. Both authentic and inauthentic acts express my freedom now in terms of my continuity with the past and my dependence upon my cultural conditioning. The freedom of the twentieth-century technocrat is quite different from the freedom of the early twentieth-century industrialist. Ford Motor Company can no longer be the private domain of Henry Ford, yet the corporation's freedom to affect the economic health of the United States is far greater than Henry Ford I ever dreamed.

That decisions are made *now,* but are at the same time not nonhistorical, has been discussed before. The time-fullness of existence not only ensures that meaningfulness is now, it also assures us that one apect of that meaningfulness is the continuity with past meaningful moments out of which our understanding (ambiguous as that is) of *this* moment arises. Again, the time-fulness of existence assures us that though our decision is *now,* that *now* will have a continuous influence upon future decisions. The commitment I make on my wedding day is part of the now-commitment I must continue making one, ten, or thirty-seven years later.

In each of these aspects of decision, one thing becomes clear: there is no such thing as the guaranteed, absolute, or final "right" decision, as any parent can affirm without analytical justification. Any decision is in some significant part a leap into the unknown, a commitment beyond proof or evidence for which we can only prepare ourselves as responsibly as possible. For the secularist, this means a responibility to self in terms of *Being;* for the religionist, it means a responsibility to self and to God. In either case, the self is involved in his community of encounter.

In terms of the New Humanism, this means that any New Morality must be a responsible expression of *Being*-in-action. Such an action begins in encounter and ends in enactment, which is another way of stating that my response begins in authenticity and ends in an affirmation grounded in freedom. The standards, laws, and goals we establish for ourselves as secularists, or in keeping with our response to God as men of faith, are always tentative and subject to change, but on the other hand authoritative and demanding of our resolute loyalty. A rational, meaningful existence demands that accuracy and clarity exist, that effective order and coherence prevail. It is the ambiguity of these norms which makes change possible, but only when the risk of rebellion seems less than the risk of meaninglessness. Such an imbalance of risks is the case when the *I-It* world assumes the authority of or priority over the *I-Thou* world, when principle becomes more important than person, law more important than love. When reform is found to be impossible, then rebellion is necessary. Albert Camus, writing about the liberation of Paris in 1944, makes this point perfectly evident:

Four years ago men rose up amid ruins and despair and calmly declared that nothing was lost. They said we had to carry on and that the forces of good could always overcome the forces of evil if we were willing to pay the price. They paid the price. And, to be sure, that price was heavy; it had all the weight of blood and the dreadful heaviness of prisons. Many of those men are dead, whereas others have been living for years surrounded by windowless walls. That was the price that had to be paid. But those same men, if they could, would not blame us for this terrible and marvelous joy that sweeps us off our feet like a high tide. For our joy has not broken faith with them. On the contrary, it justifies them and declares that they were right. . . . Nothing is given to men, and the little they can conquer is paid for with unjust deaths. But man's greatness lies elsewhere. It lies in his decision to be stronger than his condition. And if his condition is unjust, he has only one way of overcoming it, which is to be just himself.[3]

Needless to say, relatively trivial changes require commensurately trivial risks. Customs change through defiance more quickly than laws, laws more quickly than cultural myths, and cultural myths more quickly than faith or belief. For example, the risk a boy takes in defying the contemporary masculine image by wearing his hair long, growing a beard, or wearing bright colorful clothing, is really not great

—a Victorian school board or school principal may demand that he "shape up" or "ship out," or his peers may jeer that he is really a g-i-r-l. Styles and customs have always been changed by those with the courage to defy the acceptable for the sake of the new. What proves creative and expressive remains; what is simply defiant and destructive soon disappears.

Laws, on the other hand, change more slowly. They themselves are the product of established and, usually, honored customs, enacted to protect society from specific abuses. Defiance here is more costly and more complicated. The threat of official public reprimand, fine, or imprisonment usually insures that defiance is more than just a whim. Because this type of change applies to everyone, an extended example may be warranted.

In the United States, certain laws govern legalized abortion. Defiance has arisen in the form of a general disregard for the law, with one exception: the *official* Roman Catholic community. For Roman Catholics, the issue revolves about the Church's belief that "life" begins not at birth but at conception. Abortion is therefore the arbitrary taking of a life intended by God—to any Catholic, of course, a heinous sin. The act of abortion is not simply defiance of the State, it is defiance of God. Consequently, there is no pressure for change from official quarters.

For some Catholics, the majority of Protestants, and secularists, however, the situation is different. These groups recognize neither the "natural law" tradition nor any other authoritative or definitive ruling about prenatal life. Other human factors have assumed greater importance. Arguments in favor of abortion usually begin by the loaded question: "Would it not be more humane to end the existence of a foetus which has been damaged by thalidimide or German measles?" Why bring a disfigured, handicapped, or retarded child into the world when it is unnecessary, and cruel for the child? Such arguments are persuasive, but the ethical-legal problem becomes more subtle and more difficult when one anticipates a normal pregnancy.

Many concerned people believe that the life of an unwanted child is jeopardized from the beginning. If, as many child psychologists maintain, the basic attitude of the child toward the world is framed, if not fixed, within the first six months of its life, there is little weight to the counter argument that the unwanted child could win its way into the hearts of recalcitrant parents, if indeed it has "parents" to win. To believe this is to romanticize child-care in the first place, and to ignore the clinical evidence of "disturbed children" who are conditioned by such tension-situations in the second place. It might also be the case that the physical or mental health of the mother would be endangered by pregnancy and birth, a situation for which abortion is the obvious solution. Fortunately, some parts of the world already acknowledge this condition as reason enough for the operation. Or it may be the case that the two people involved in the conception are truly not in love and should not be married. Perhaps they are simply too young for marriage. Must placing the child up for adoption be the only way out?

These and a host of similar "humane" considerations compel people to seek out an illegal abortionist who, for several hundred dollars or more, "takes care of things." If one is not convinced that the official Roman Catholic position concerning the beginning of "life" can be maintained, then the case for possible abortion can be reasonably argued in terms of the merits surrounding each individual situation, so that the result may truly represent that affirmation of life characteristic of the New Humanism. If life is here-and-now, and life is threatened by a pregnancy which is determined deleterious to those involved, then one hopes that laws (which are to protect life) will enable abortion to occur. To deny it categorically under any conditions others than those official Roman Catholicism has established, would seem far too restrictive and punitive. If the reason for denial is that the participants were "bad" or irresponsible and should pay for their folly, then such a primitive denial is not responsive— and, perhaps psychologically irresponsible—to the situation and is possibly sadistic. Nor should abortion be denied because then "everyone would do it"—as though it were done for a lark at lunchtime break. No one who has agonized over the decision, had the standard "dilation and curettage," experienced the emotional strain, and paid the bill, believes it to be so inconsequential.

The above arguments are incomplete, oversimplified, and themselves riddled with ambiguity; but they do at least give some sense of the dilemmas that many people face. Such dilemmas, in turn, provide motivation for action, both legal and illegal, which could change the laws of a nation. The price of such change is high; but the price of no change is higher. It cannot be otherwise for life characterized by ambiguity, for meaning dependent upon encounter here-and-now.

The change in cultural myths or ethos, e.g., the change from a rural mentality to an urban mentality in America, is even more complicated, more risky, more costly, and more lengthy. The technical and financial crises in the major cities of the world are only one phase of the great human problem caused by the change. Politicians whose responsibility it is to administer city governments know the problems in terms of power, representation, and financial apportionments on the local, state, and federal levels. But we all know that there are poignant human problems involving poverty, waste, exploitation, hunger, and so forth, where the risk of the search for meaning has become worth the risk of defiance.

Responsible organizational leaders of American minority groups—Charles Evers, Roy Wilkins, Cesar Chavez—and responsible government advisors—Sargent Shriver, Abraham Ribicoff, Otto Kerner—all suggest that it would take a crash program involving tens of billions of dollars to begin to rectify the hardships and inequities of a technological society trying to function with a rural mind-set. Unfortunately, as we have observed, even in such enlightened cities as New Haven, Connecticut, money—even were it available—is not enough. In terms of law, it means constitutional revisions; in terms of society, it means a redistribution of power, apportionments, and aid programs. None of this can happen without working hardships on the existing Establishment or at least depriving it of its position of authority and importance. Such a transition cannot take place without struggle and without changes of heart and mind in the citizenry itself. Money cannot buy peace for long and can never provide meaning. The recent organization of militant poverty groups, of Black Power groups, and their concomitant refusal of Establishment help and Establishment dollars are all evidences of the colossal struggle going on in the United States. One can only hope, in spite of grave doubts, that reforms will come quickly and reasonably enough that the risk for meaning will not necessitate any greater acts of defiance. Such is the tension of cultural ambiguity which necessarily and continuously juxtaposes one's responsibilities to the *It* and *Thou* worlds.

The change in faith and belief is even more traumatic, for here the point of our orientation, the very center of meaning, is shaken. Despite the fact that we recognize and know the ambiguity of belief, we resist such changes with great tenacity. The change in belief means not only a change in our understanding of *Being* or God, but also a consequent change in our own identity. Is it any wonder, then, that men and women of the older generations, set in their religious ways, become the conservatives of the community? Superior wisdom does not make them so adament; their fear of change, loss of power, loss of understanding, and loss of meaning does. Is it any wonder that the recent innovations initiated by the Second Vatican Council and by the theological turmoil within Protestantism have produced powerful reactions among all churchmen, laymen and clergy alike? For some, the changes are signs of apostasy—sin in its most subtle form; for others, these changes signal the rebirth without which Christianity is a quaint cultural curiosity. Not since the reformation itself has the Church experienced such change. It is our privilege and peril to live in an age when the need for meaning has produced radical reforms. But, radical reforms in religious expression take generations for effective assimilation. Meanwhile, they occasion profound spiritual anxiety which is often expressed as massive resistance to change.

We are concerned here with all of these changes. We are engaged in a genuine search for a new sense of our humanity and a more relevant morality. The old lights have gone out; the old gods have died; the old ways are inadequate. Life lived meaningfully in the *now*, in terms of our *Being* or in terms of our God, is beginning to emerge, but the patterns are not yet distinct. What is distinct, however, is the overall pattern which includes the presence of the ambiguity of encounter. It is something like this that I believe E. E. Cummings had in mind when he wrote:

> are world's collapsing? any was a glove
> but i'm and you are actual either hand
> is when for sale? forever is to give
> and on forever's very now we stand[4]

Thus the delicate balance is sought between structure and freedom, stability and change. As in any fragile human situation, too much weight on one side brings a compensatory reaction to restore the ambiguity necessary for free and meaningful human existence. The danger is that the compensation will be excessive: too much structure brings too much indeterminism; too much objectivity results in too much subjectivism; too much order invites too much chaos. The times in which we live, on all the levels we have discussed, exhibit such contending forces as indeterminism, subjectivism, and irrationality. But, in the gradual emergence of the New Humanism, order and reason will again begin to reassert their authority hopefully, creatively, freely, and affirmatively, yet never absolutely. The awareness of ambiguity adds a new dimension to our understanding of our responsibility for life here-and-now.

The humanist revolution in the arts, in philosophy, and in religion is really an expression of man's authenticity. He takes the risk of defying both inhuman absolutism and ahuman chaos in order to establish communities of meaning. In such communities, *Being* can express itself freely in the integrity of its own existence or in its acknowledgment of the love of God. Within such communities, relative standards of value and behavior exist and are changed only through risk and cost. And such costs must be paid. For such communities the meaningfulness of the moment is the ground of genuine eventfulness, the recognition of the importance of the fullness of the present, of history, of time.

That such meaningfulness points beyond itself to some final resolution is an assertion of faith, not of knowledge. Ambiguity permits no finality. Consequently such issues remain secondary for the New Morality. What does concern us is the quality of lives we determine within the determining context. For the secularist, that is enough. For the man of faith, if heaven—some new context of *Being*—be the later wish of God, so be it. Meaning is not then. It is *now*.

Notes

CHAPTER 1

1   Paul Goodman, as quoted by *Time Magazine*, April 22, 1966, p. 42.

2   *The Complete Works of Friedrich Nietzsche*, ed. Dr. Oscar Levy, Vol. 10, *The Joyful Wisdom*, (New York, Russell and Russell, Inc., 1964), Section 125, p. 167ff.

3   *New York Times*, April 13, 1967.

4   Jack Newfield, "Revolt without Dogma," *Motive*, October, 1965, p. 21.

5   *New York Times*, April 23, 1967, p. 20.

6   Arthur Miller, *After the Fall*, The Viking Press, New York, 1964, pp. 3–4.

CHAPTER 2

1   Edgar Friedenberg, "A Polite Encounter between the Generations," *New York Times Magazine*, January 16, 1966, p. 72.

2   Stephen Spender, *The Struggle of the Modern*, University of California Press, Berkeley, 1963, p. 154.

3   J. W. Kvitch, "Creative Dilemma," *Saturday Review*, February, 1964, p. 17.

4 As quoted by Gibson Danes, "Freedom and Responsibility," *Looking at Modern Painting*, Eureka Press, Los Angeles, 1957, p. 89.

5 As quoted by G. R. Swenson, "What Is Pop Art?" *Art News*, November, 1963, p. 25.

6 *Ibid.*, p. 27.

7 As quoted by Peter Selz, *German Expressionist Painting*, University of California Press, Berkeley, Calif., 1957, p. 202.

8 *Ibid.*, pp. 202–203.

9 *Ibid.*, p. 220.

10 *Ibid.*, p. 210.

11 *Ibid.*, p. 226.

12 Selden Rodman, *The Insiders*, Louisiana State University Press, Baton Rouge, 1960, p. 34.

13 *Ibid.*, p. 74.

14 Paul Klee, *On Modern Art*, translated by Paul Findlay, Faber & Faber, Ltd., London, 1948, p. 49.

15 George Biddle, *The Yes and No of Contemporary Art*, Harvard University Press, Cambridge, Mass., 1957, p. 111.

16 Frank O'Hara (ed.), *Robert Motherwell*, Doubleday & Company, Inc., Garden City, N. Y., 1965, p. 58.

17 As quoted by W. W. Austin, *Music in the 20th Century*, W. W. Norton & Co., Inc., New York, 1966, p. 204.

18 As quoted by Marion Baner, *Twentieth Century Music*, G. P. Putnam's Sons, New York, 1933, pp. 211–212, (from W. Kandinsky's *The Art of Spiritual Harmony*, translated with Introduction by M. T. H. Sadler).

19 Igor Stravinsky, *Autobiography*, Steuer, New York, 1958, pp. 53–54.

20 Igor Stravinsky, *Poetics of Music in the Form of Six Lessons*, translated by Arthur Knodel and Ingolf Dahl, Harvard University Press, Cambridge, Mass., 1947.

21 Richard Kostelanetz, "Two Extremes of Avant-Garde Music," *New York Times Magazine*, January, 1967, pp. 34–35.

22 John Cage, *Silence*, Wesleyan University Press, Middletown, Conn., 1961, p. 52.

23 *Ibid.*, p. 95.

24 As quoted by Aaron Copland, *Our New Music*, Whittlesey House, McGraw-Hill Book Company, New York, 1941, pp. 107–108.

25 Peter Yates, *Twentieth Century Music*, Pantheon Books, Random House, Inc., New York, 1967, p. 268.

26 Richard Ellmann and Charles Feidelson, Jr. (eds.), *The Modern Tradition*, Oxford University Press, Fairlawn, N. J., 1965.

27 Edmund Wilson, *Axel's Castle*, Charles Scribner's Sons, New York, 1931, p. 2.

28 Maurice Friedman, *Problematic Rebel*, Random House, Inc., New York, 1963, p. viii.

29 Herman Melville, *Moby Dick*, Dodd, Mead & Company, Inc., New York, 1923, pp. 147–148.

30 Fyodor Dostoyevsky, "Notes from Underground," *The Short Novels of Dostoyevsky*, Dial Press, New York, 1945, p. 132.

31 Wilson, *op. cit.*, p. 21.

32 Franz Kafka, "The Metamorphosis," translated by A. L. Lloyd, Vanguard Press, Inc., New York, 1946, pp. 11–12.

33 Wilson, *op. cit.*, pp. 255–256.

34 Albert Camus, *The Fall*, Vintage Books, Random House, Inc., New York, 1963, p. 50.

35 *Ibid.*, pp. 6–7.

36 Archibald MacLeish, *J.B.*, Sentry Edition, Houghton Mifflin Company, Boston, 1961, p. 49.

37 *Ibid.*

38 Ihab Hassan, "The Way Down and Out," *Virginia Quarterly Review*, Winter, 1963, p. 93.

39 Paul Carroll, Interview by David Ossman, *The Sullan Art*, Corinth Books, New York, 1963, pp. 20–21.

40 John Logan, Interview by David Ossman, *ibid.*, pp. 43–44.

41 LeRoi Jones, Interview by David Ossman, *ibid.*, p. 79.

42 Alan Lewis, *American Plays and Playwrights*, Crown Publishers, Inc., New York, 1965, p. 257.

43 Marcus Klein, *After Alienation: American Novels in Mid-Century*, The World Publishing Company, Cleveland, 1964.

CHAPTER 3

1 Soren Kierkegaard, *The Concluding Unscientific Postscript*, translated by David F. Swenson, Princeton University Press, Princeton, N. J., 1941, pp. 97–98.

2 Martin Buber, *Between Man and Man*, translated by Ronald Gregor Smith, Routledge and Kegan Paul, London, 1947, p. 177.

3 *Ibid.*, p. 168.

4 *Ibid.*, p. 171.

5 *Ibid.*, p. 166

6 Martin Buber, *I and Thou*, translated by Ronald Gregor Smith, T. & T. Clark, Edinburgh, 1937, p. 34.

7 *Ibid.*, p. 79.

8 *Ibid.*, p. 67.

9 *Ibid.*, p. 63.

10 *Ibid.*, p. 65.

11 *Ibid.*, pp. 14–15.

CHAPTER 4

1 Lewis Mumford, *The Arts in Renewal*, University of Pennsylvania Press, Philadelphia, 1951, pp. 30–31.

2 As quoted by Harry T. Moore, *Contemporary American Novelists*, Southern Illinois University Press, Carbondale, 1964, p. xx.

3 Paris Leary and Robert Kelly (eds.), *A Controversy of Poets*, Anchor Books, Doubleday and Company, Inc., Garden City, New York, 1965, p. 319.

4 *Ibid.*, p. 190.

5 Alan Paton, *Cry, the Beloved Country*, Charles Scribner's Sons, New York, 1948, pp. 170–171.

6 Albert Camus, *Resistance, Rebellion, and Death*, translated by Justin O'Brien, Alfred A. Knopf, Inc., New York, 1961, pp. 240–241.

7 *Ibid.*, pp. 266–267.

8 Dorothy Tuck (ed.), *Crowell's Handbook of Faulkner*, Thomas Y. Crowell Company, New York, 1964, p. 244.

CHAPTER 5

1 Matt. 11:27b R.S.V. translation.

2 Gen. 3:56 R.S.V. translation.

3 Fyodor Dostoyevsky, *op. cit.*, pp. 147–148.

4 Finley Eversole, *Christian Faith and the Contemporary Arts*, Abingdon Press, Nashville, Tenn., 1962, p. 46.

5   As quoted by Selden Rodman, *op. cit.*, p. 82.

6   As quoted by Peter Yates, *op. cit.*, p. 109.

7   As quoted by Frank O'Hara, *op. cit.*, p. 47.

8   John Cage, *Silence, op. cit.*, p. 94.

CHAPTER 6

1   H. Richard Niebuhr, *The Responsible Self*, Harper & Row, Publishers, Incorporated, New York, 1963, p. 140.

2   H. Richard Niebuhr, *Christ and Culture*, Harper & Row, Publishers, Incorporated, New York, 1951, pp. 12–13.

CHAPTER 7

1   Reinhold Niebuhr, *The Children of Light and the Children of Darkness*, Nisbet and Company, Ltd., London, p. vi.

2   H. Richard Niebuhr, *Christ and Culture*, Harper & Row, Incorporated, New York, p. 234.

3   Albert Camus, *Resistance, Rebellion, and Death*, translated by Justin, O'Brien, Alfred A. Knopf, Inc., New York, 1961, pp. 38–40.

4   E. E. Cummings, "what freedom's not some under's mere above," 100 *Selected Poems*, Grove Press, Inc., New York, p. 84.

Index

THE PILL, the death of God, civil disobedience, and legalized abortion are common
topics in modern America. They serve to
illustrate the contemporary challenge to
our traditional standards and morals
honored in the pre-World War I years.
Modern technology has had its triumphs,
but not without exacting a price. Once the
goal was to glorify God and enjoy Him
forever; now it appears to be to glorify
life and enjoy it as long as possible. Modern man has been left bewildered, confused, and purposeless. Modern man must
find new values before despair and suicide
destroy him and his world.

Charles Ketcham incisively describes
the decline of older values and clearly
assesses our present quandary. We can
either turn to a technological amoralism,
escape into mysticism, or accept the invi-
tation to creatively participate in the evo-
lution of a New Age, a New Humanism.
Only the last of these alternatives can
lead to a meaningful, viable civilization.

Dr. Ketcham examines the implications
which new movements in art, music, literature, and philosophy have for the twentieth century. Despite the seeming chaos
and nihilism caused by the breakdown of
traditional forms, he recognizes positive
values in these new movements. The core
of the book is a humanistic synthesis of